Growing Roses

SMALL GARDEN LIBRARY

Growing Roses

Jack L. Harkness

with photographs by Betty Harkness

Studio Vista

Published in 1967 by Studio Vista Limited
Blue Star House, Highgate Hill, London N19

Distributed in Canada by General Publishing Company Limited
30 Lesmill Road, Don Mills, Ontario

Set and printed in 10 pt Imprint

Made and printed in Great Britain by
The Garden City Press Limited
Letchworth, Hertfordshire

TO

OLIVIA AMY HARKNESS

I always promised my mother
that the first book I wrote
should be dedicated to her.
I never thought, but she did,
that the time would occur.
I am here to see it, she is not.
It is a small return for all her
love, but I make it with all of
mine.

Contents

List of Illustrations

1 *Roses are the best plants to grow*

This book has one purpose: to be a truthful and reliable friend of anyone who wants to make a garden of roses. Everything contained is essential to this end, and nothing is superfluous, apart from digressions for our mutual amusement, which are a temptation I have no intention of resisting.

Most people pick up a book, wondering if it will answer their needs, thus unconsciously testing the integrity of author and publisher. If it is openly admitted that a book is of no use to any but, for example, students of thirteenth-century sewage disposal, then a large number of potential customers will lose interest at the outset. It is therefore more usual to advertise a book as being vital to the entire community, in the hope that the greater part of the population will have paid their money and read into Chapter Three before fully realizing they are studying serfs and villeins digging drains.

No such duplicity shall flourish here. This book is written for the Reluctant Gardener, the Wife-Persuaded Gardener, and the Wish-I-Knew-the-First-Thing Gardener. It is a Primer, not a Treatise. Learned experts may quite possibly disapprove of it. It tells you how to make your garden the easy way. That is why it is about roses.

I picture the Reluctant Gardener, anxious to transform into a miniature Eden the rubble-strewn wilderness passed on to him by the builder. Or counting up the man-hours (due for deduction from his spare time) that will pass painfully in the 'matured garden' extolled by the estate agent. In gloom he foresees it will be watered with his own sweat. Deck chair, hammock will beckon in vain, for he will always be toiling, never catching up. 'This blessed plot' assumes a significance Shakespeare would never have thought of.

That situation can be avoided. Picture the other side of the coin. Sensible planning, some initial and well directed toil, and then a garden of roses—fresh, tidy, fragrant. You stir in your deck chair, turn over another page, and as you hear your neighbours slaving, a slow smile of content breaks over your face, and you charitably resolve to tell them about this book, rehearsing in your mind the great virtues of the rose.

Gardens are made for many reasons, of which the most common

are a desire for a peaceful environment; a love of beauty; a wish to increase the value of the property; and the search for a healthy and rewarding hobby.

We live in prosperous times, when the modest amount of money needed to make a garden, either complete or by degrees, is no undue burden to the finances of the average family. But our prosperous times are also very busy times. The more leisure we get, the less time we have. A garden which becomes a burden of labour is no use to anyone. It must be quickly and easily maintained. This is all the more important to us when the years reduce our physical energy.

Roses meet all the requirements we have set forth in the two preceding paragraphs.

Roses create a peaceful environment. A child seeing a rambler in full flower will carry in his mind for ever those clouds upon clouds of blossom stretching up to the blue sky. Moving among your roses in the cool of the day, you will know a quiet pleasure and satisfaction, deep as any other possession, save perhaps your home itself, can give you.

Roses gratify the longing for beauty in the same way as a great work of art. On a more material plane, roses are an investment, making your property more pleasing to yourself and your neighbours. If you should wish to sell your house, a good rose garden will push the price up.

As a hobby, rose growing is healthy, taking one out of doors. It is not hard work, once the initial preparation is done, and it is certainly rewarding, for roses give outstanding results.

No kind of gardening, short of putting the whole lot down to concrete, is as quick, easy and cheap to maintain as a rose garden.

These are the compelling and sufficient reasons for growing roses. Now let us look closer, still in general terms, at the nature of the plant we are studying.

The rose is hardy, able to stand our English winters. Losses from winter freezing are very rare. No need to frown upon the Christmas turkey, worrying about the roses in the snow. They are not like softer plants, neither wilting, dying nor importuning their owner for protection. They are perfectly happy in the snow. Their owner can enjoy his Christmas dinner without a care in the world.

The rose is long lived, although life expectation is not the same for every variety. Given proper care, a rose tree will live for many years. Cautiously, a nurseryman will suggest ten or fifteen years.

Exuberantly, people who grow roses well, report life-spans of twenty-five to forty years.

Beauty, it is said, is in the eye of the beholder. Beholders are unanimous in finding the rose a thing of beauty and a joy for ever. One will praise their most varied scent. Another will praise the colours; roses are as changeable as sunsets: summer colour and autumn colour different; young colour and old colour different; rain colour and drought colour different. As the human face can change from smiles to tears, so rose colours are expressive, changing in answer to the moods of nature. But rose colours have one unfailing virtue; they are brilliant. Many flowers are dull beside the rose.

Of all the delicate attributes which make a rose, the one I value most is its form. The intricate ravellings of the petals, the symmetry sculptured by nature, the sureness of positioning no drawing board could achieve—here is the crowning glory of the rose. It is as telling and lovely in a five-petalled single flower as in a hundred-petalled double one. A rose without form is a poor dud, like an empty bottle of beer to a thirsty man.

The rose is generous with its flowers. That is the final and greatest reason for its popularity. It gives a massive display of bloom, repeatedly, so that the owner of a rose garden can hardly find himself without a flower from early June to Christmas Day.

These are the reasons why roses are the best plants to grow. Next, we must study our subject more closely before we start work. An artist considers his paints before brush daubs canvas; we will now study the genus *Rosa* before we lay out our rose garden.

2 *A survey of the genus* Rosa

All we need to know at present is the material from which our rose garden will be made. We are not particularly interested whether the roses are Bourbons, Spinosissimas or Hybrid Gorgonzolas. This classification business is violently overdone, because it is based partly on parentage, which is largely unknown, and partly on characteristics, which mingle and merge inconveniently, thus frustrating the would-be classifier.

Let us then adopt the Philistine but commonsense and practical course of dividing roses by approximate height. Thus we shall know their scope for planning, and learn something of the classes that matter at the same time.

Not that height is a foolproof division of roses. Even as in colour they smile and frown, so in height they rise or stoop unexpectedly. Height is the key to good planning, yet any plan based on it must accept the jokes of nature. Gardening is full of surprises, for nature likes to put man in his place when he is ordering her about. We must accept the surprises with a good grace, like the lass at the bridge table who said to her furious partner, 'But I think counting the trumps spoils the element of surprise in the game.'

Our survey starts with the lowest roses, and gradually rises up to the strongest climbers, where only mountaineer greenfly dare go. If I am rash enough to state heights, they are hereby qualified 'Give or take a bit according to conditions'.

Group I—ankle high

The smallest roses grow less than 12ins in height. They are called miniature roses. This does not mean that you can pick up a nurseryman's catalogue, order any of his list of miniatures, and receive plants of uniform height. Far from it! You will find 'Peon' ('Tom Thumb'), 'Rouletti', 'Sweet Fairy' and 'Humpty-Dumpty' are tiny, less than 6ins tall. These very small miniatures are of limited use in the garden; any but the keen sighted wielding a hoe will probably consign them to the rubbish heap along with the weeds. So it is a waste of money to buy them unless we have exactly the right place for them. Sentimental people who see them at shows, and plant them among the Michaelmas daisies, might just as well put their money on a three-legged horse entered for the Derby by the Bookmakers' Association. There is a special place in the open garden for these little fellows, in holes left in a retaining wall against soil, where they can sprout out of the stone-work prettily; or on little ledges of soil, built up above ground level; and in small pockets of soil left in, or by, pathways.

Group II—over your ankles

About 12ins high are most of the other miniatures; some of them are narrow, spindly plants, useful for the same kind of purposes as the little ones just mentioned. Such are 'Baby Faurax', 'Baby Gold Star', 'Rosina', 'Cinderella', 'New Penny', 'Perla de Montserrat', 'Princesita' ('Pixie'). But others are exuberant and bushy, growing out as wide as they are tall, and consequently they are first-rate edging plants. 'Baby Masquerade', 'Pour Toi' and 'Perla de Alcanada' are outstanding examples. True miniature roses have thin stems, small leaves and flowers, all the parts being scaled down to size. A short growing rose with large leaves and blooms is not a Miniature Rose but a stunted rose. Of this nature, and in this height group, are the Compacta Roses, whose original German names were changed to those of Snow White's Seven Dwarfs à la Disney—Grumpy, Sleepy, etc!

Group III—shin high

Up another step we go, to look at the roses in the region of 12 to 18ins high. I regret to inform you that we shall still find miniature roses! 'Bit O' Sunshine', 'Little Flirt', 'Robin', 'Colibri' are all very pretty, and may be used as edging plants; or as tall groups behind shorter miniatures; or as short groups in front of other varieties. Into this height range enter a few other types. We meet the lowest Floribunda Roses, such as 'Summer Song' and 'Marlena'; there will be many new ones like these coming from the breeders in the near future.

The word 'Floribunda' describes a Bush Rose, which achieves ts greatest glory by bringing out on each main stem many flowers simultaneously. If you try to express it more precisely, you run into the difficulties that classifiers know, for nature does not divide herself into groups. She is an individualist, literally down to the tips of our fingers.

Still in the same range are the lower growing Dwarf Polyantha

Roses, or to use their strange official title, Polyantha Pompons. These titles supposedly indicate their origin, height and flower form; but they have different origins, different heights and different flower forms. We only need to note that they are useful little roses for edges, for narrow borders, for any place where we may need this height. 'Margo Koster', 'Éblouissant', and 'Jean Mermoz' are the best. Finally there is 'Cecile Brunner', the 'Sweetheart Rose', spindly in growth, but with adorable little flowers.

Group IV—knee high

Next, the Floribundas begin to come into their own, such free-flowering kinds as 'Paddy McGredy', 'Golden Jewel', 'Golden Slippers', 'Lilac Charm', 'Sarabande', 'Dusky Maiden', 'Goldilocks', 'Meteor', 'Nathalie Nypels', 'Yvonne Rabier'. The taller Dwarf Polyanthas (which were in past years used as Floribundas are to-day) are of similar height; the most famous is 'Gloire du Midi' (or 'Gloria Mundi'); and many similar varieties exist, mutations of Orleans Rose and of one another, 'Paul Crampel', 'Rufus', 'Miss Edith Cavell', 'Conchita,' 'Cameo', 'Coral Cluster' and 'Little Dorrit' being perhaps the most famous. They are all prone to mildew; they are the true 'pom-poms'. Related, but different, having life-sap from other species, are 'Katharina Zeimet', 'Ellen Poulsen', 'Sheelagh Baird' and 'Mrs Joseph Hiess'. These are healthy, and would put you in mind of ramblers flowering on little bushes. A treasure from 1879, very rare, but most individual and lovely, is 'Little White Pet', one of those varieties which makes your rose parden different from the one next door, and gives pleasure far beyond the proportions of its limited yet decisive habit of growth. Finally we should mention Viridiflora, the green rose, its flower parts nothing but partly modified leaves, a suitable candidate for the 'Ugh!' corner, should we want one.

Notice the richness and variety of the genus *Rosa*. Already we have a diversity of habit, form and colour in each height surveyed. We will study the habit when we are planning; the form and colour when we think of the best varieties. All will be made plain, but meanwhile, let us see what we have a little taller.

Group V—over your knees

Now the Hybrid Teas enter the field. Here are the aristocrats of the rose world, worthy of a better title; the difference between

Floribunda and Hybrid Tea grows smaller each year, for the virtues of both are gradually being combined in one plant. Hybrid Teas and Floribundas flower for much the same period of time; it is not true, though commonly believed, that Floribundas never stop blooming. They take their rest. We can assume for our purposes that Hybrid Teas have larger, more perfect flowers, and show their greatest glory in the perfection of a single bloom upon a thorny stem.

The shorter growing Hybrid Teas interest us now. We find 'Beauté', 'Belle Blonde', 'Bettina', 'Dorothy Peach', 'Fragrant Cloud', 'McGredy's Ivory', 'McGredy's Yellow', 'Mme Louis Laperrière', 'Miss Ireland', 'Mrs Sam McGredy', 'Picture'—a dear old friend this. The ever fresh 'Shot Silk', 'Pink Favourite', 'Violinista Costa', 'Virgo', the white rose. Of similar height are many Floribundas, the shorter and neater of their kind. 'Allgold', that superb yellow; 'Anna Wheatcroft', 'Celebration', 'Chanelle', 'Circus', ('The Greatest Rose Show on Earth', said the raisers), 'Dearest', 'Decapo', 'Dickson's Flame', 'Elizabeth of Glamis', 'Europeana', 'Fashion' and 'Red Favourite'. These Hybrid Teas and Floribundas are the staple varieties for beds and borders where we desire neat, compact growth. Many of them are most particularly suitable as a low hedge ruling the margin of a drive or pathway.

Group VI—thigh high

We do not wish to stoop low to smell our roses, especially as the years pass and backs grow stiff. It is therefore convenient to allow them to grow up to about 36ins, a good height for viewing the flowers.

Many of the finest Hybrid Teas and Floribundas oblige us by growing in this way. 'Ena Harkness', 'Ballet', 'Crimson Glory', 'Golden Melody', and 'Grand'mère Jenny'; 'Josephine Bruce' and 'Lady Sylvia'; 'Memoriam', 'Mischief', 'Mojave', 'My Choice' and 'Ophelia'; 'Perfecta', 'Piccadilly', 'Silver Lining', 'Stella'; all these are good Hybrid Teas. Of Floribundas, 'Alain', 'August Seebauer', 'Columbine', 'Jiminy Cricket', (the only rose, I believe, to be named in honour of a fictional insect), 'Lilli Marlene', 'Moulin Rouge', 'Orangeade', 'Orange Sensation', 'Paprika', 'Pink Parfait', 'Rumba' and 'Sweet Repose'.

Several interesting roses of other types grow to this height too. *R. gallica versicolor* (Rosa Mundi) is a pink flower striped with white. It flowers very little after its summer flush, and like most

old stagers of this kind, goes off sick in August and September
with mildew. It is a little piece of history, for it was grown in
Shakespeare's day, and nobody knows how long before that.
'Penelope' is usually described as a Hybrid Musk, a classification
which if possible is less reliable than those we have already mentioned. We may picture Hybrid Musks as Floribundas of more
robust growth—'Penelope' is on the short side for its type; but it
makes quite a large shrub laterally, smothers itself with semi-
double blush-white flowers, broadcasts a light and pleasant
fragrance, and is quite content to settle down to produce a
fantastic burden of seed pods unless we cut them off and make it
flower again.

'The Fairy' may play tricks with us, for it is capable of growing
taller than 3ft and equally of remaining shorter. It is in fact the
bush form of the rambler 'Lady Godiva' (which a nurseryman once
succinctly described as 'flesh'). It flowers in such profusion that
the stems tend to arch. The Moss Rose, 'William Lobb', has rosy-
purple flowers, very striking. Moss Roses take their name from
the strange mossy growth on the calyx and sepals. Most of them
are not spectacular in flower, just interesting. 'William Lobb' is
the most remarkable in flower, but rather short on moss. Little
autumn flower is to be expected on Moss Roses.

One more class has a solitary representative here; in Nelson's
days, many varieties were selected from the wild Scotch Rose, a
prickly, small-leafed briar. They formed a large and important
section among the roses of that period. In 1838, a blush-white
variety appeared, with the remarkable ability of flowering again
in the autumn. It is 'Stanwell Perpetual'; thorny, briar-like, compact—and pretty.

Group VII—hip high

If we wish to have our roses generally taller, or if, owing to
unpromising conditions, we think it necessary to use varieties of
extra vigour, we will find an excellent selection. Splendid Hybrid
Teas offer themselves—'Gail Borden' (one of the best in rain);
'Helen Traubel', 'Karl Herbst', 'King's Ransom', 'Montezuma',
'Opera', 'Prima Ballerina'—we must stop a minute at that one,
because it smells like a perfume shop—'Rose Gaujard', 'Spek's
Yellow', 'Summer Sunshine' and one of the very greatest of all,
'Super Star'; 'Sutter's Gold' and 'Wendy Cussons', both frag-
rant, the latter a very successful English rose. Some of the best
Floribundas enter this height range too: 'Highlight', 'Honey-

moon'—but let us take notice of one of the finest roses ever seen, the superb 'Iceberg'. Grown as an individual bush, it flowers on the top and round the sides as well; in a bed, it gives three flushes of bloom in the time others give two. May 'Iceberg' never melt! To continue, 'Korona', 'Masquerade', 'Red Dandy', 'Shepherd's Delight', 'Spartan', 'Vera Dalton' and 'Woburn Abbey'.

Less common kinds must be mentioned too. 'Blanc Double de Coubert', for one, a very worthy French variety which has hung in the catalogues since 1892. It is a Rugosa Rose, that is, developed from the species of that name, and as a dutiful child, it carries the influence of its parents, in shiny, thick leaves and bristle-covered stems. This is the purest white there is in roses, and the scent is good. The flowers are spoiled by rain, but the leaves are very fine, usually the first to start growing in spring. This tough and trouble-free rose makes a thorny, wide shrub, and most nurserymen carry a small stock of it to please the minority who want it. Once, many years ago, a letter to *The Times* praised highly its virtues as a hedge, for which it is indeed well suited. Surprised nurserymen, few of whom read *The Times*, began to receive orders for 'Blanc Double de Coubert'—not in the accustomed ones or twos, but in twelves, fifties, hundreds. I fear that few of those hedges were ever planted—the stock was insufficient. Nurserymen patiently propagated 'Blanc Double de Coubert' in greater numbers for the following year, and sat back hoping they would have enough. Alas, they were too late; readers of *The Times* were engrossed in other matters, and this hedging rose so amazing and necessary twelve months before, was now quite forgotten.

Many old-fashioned roses qualify for mention too. But let me first give a word of warning. Nineteenth-century roses have much the same relation to modern roses as a stage-coach has to a Rolls-Royce, or candles to electric light. They are charming, interesting, beautiful, and then come the disadvantages. Their dull foliage looks tired in July and white with mildew for the rest of the summer (you don't know what mildew is until you see them!). The flowering season is sweet but short. I think that one of the most lovely is 'Mme Pierre Oger', of shell-like petals and bowl-shaped flower, just made to consort with the dainty bric-à-brac of a Victorian apartment. It is classed as a Bourbon Rose in some catalogues, but as very few people can agree what a Bourbon Rose is, it is apt to turn up under other classes as well, and I daresay if you hunted back through enough publications you could find it attributed to a dozen different classes.

Group VIII—waist high

It is becoming apparent that we have no shortage of choice, as we proceed to the varieties a little taller. They will give us a commanding bed, or cover a low fence, or provide height in a mixed border. We are running out of Hybrid Teas, but a few remain, 'Eden Rose' for example, 'Gold Crown', 'John S. Armstrong', and the glorious 'Peace'. 'President Hoover' is not only tall, but long lived. Floribundas to match are 'Ann Elizabeth', 'Frensham', 'Scarlet Queen Elizabeth', 'Sea Pearl'. There is another Rugosa Rose, a little taller than 'Blanc Double de Coubert' which we mentioned in the last group. It bears the unattractive name of *R. scabrosa*, and it can make quite a big plant, 5ft or more wide. The flowers are single, luminous purple, very large, strongly scented, and they change into heps the colour of tomatoes. I had a plant of scabrosa once, which produced its first flower on Easter Saturday, and excepting for a period of two weeks' holiday for which I cannot vouch, there was at least one flower on that plant every single day until Michaelmas. It was quite a large specimen, and gave winter quarters to several thousand ladybirds. I was really sorry to leave it behind when we moved.

'Marchenland' is not a popular rose, because its flowers are similar to apple blossoms. It has pendulous stems, and looks like an arrested snow-storm, blushing at being caught in midsummer. It is variously listed as Floribunda, Hybrid Musk, or just Shrub Rose. We should mention the Hybrid Musk, 'Buff Beauty', and the near relation to the Rugosas, 'Schneezwerg'.

Group IX —chest high

Taller bushes can have their uses for hedges, screens, or just as a vertical sheet of colour, and in the 4 to 5ft range, we have a splendid Hybrid Tea in 'Buccaneer'. This can indeed be grown as a climber, and one plant so used, will produce hundreds of yellow roses in a season. 'Tally-Ho' and 'Uncle Walter' are two more upstanding Hybrid Teas, but they both tend to flower at the top of the tree. At this height we have a famous rose in 'Queen Elizabeth'. It is classified Floribunda, but that is misleading, and in America they invented a new class for it, namely Grandiflora. Here is the almost perfect hedge rose, upright, yet broad enough to screen, easy to grow, abundant in flower. Who would sweat at privet with shears when he can surround himself with 'Queen Elizabeth'?

If we need a wider hedge, the Hybrid Musk 'Cornelia' can provide it, or the double yellow Shrub Rose 'Chinatown' (Floribunda, say some: don't mix it with 'Allgold', it is twice as high and three times as thick. Floribunda indeed! I ask you!). 'Prosperity' is a Hybrid Musk with upright growth and sweet white flowers, very nice on a fence.

Group X—head high

At 5 to 6ft we have Shrub Roses which can be grown individually, or in mixed shrub borders, or as hedges. 'Bonn' (alleged Hybrid Musk) is orange-scarlet—rather crude for my taste, but at least you can see it. My own dear love at this height is 'Canary Bird', a wild rose from China and Korea. It flowers in April or May only, with single yellow roses all along its branches. Dainty in flower stem and leaf, it is the first swallow of the rose summer, and I would not be without it. 'Frau Karl Druschki' is the famous white Hybrid Tea, one of the old school, outgrowing the newcomers, and the rain inflicts a penalty on it for its presumption. 'Heidelberg' is a fine crimson Shrub Rose, and 'Joseph's Coat' is worth a place for its bright yellow and red. 'Nevada' is an interesting rose, a broad arching shrub which covers plenty of space and crams white single flowers into every inch, with a satisfactory if less generous repeat performance. 'Golden Showers', though sold as a climber, needs a lot of encouragement to exceed 6ft. 'Lady Curzon' is worth note if you like a large and perfect single rose. 'Old Pink Moss' should be mentioned as a good representative of its class. 'Frühlingsgold' is quite spectacular in May and June, flowerless thereafter.

Group XI—getting out of reach

Taking a longer stride this time, we examine varieties from 6 to 10ft. To look at the Shrub Roses first, 'Cantabrigiensis' is cream, flowering as 'Canary Bird' does, and only in late spring. *R. moyesii* has a remarkable single scarlet flower, and very fine heps, although I cannot say it ever strikes me as being completely successful; there is a lack of grace about the plant. The Sweet Briars are exactly what they are named, briars, and the kind of accommodation they require can be assessed by walking round hedges in the country and inspecting briars. It is rather pleasant to grow one for the scent of the leaves on a damp summer evening, and an excellent answer is to plant 'Lord Penzance' where he can't grow very well, thus keeping him within bounds. The flowers are so fleeting they do not matter. 'Variegata di Bologna' really needs support as it cannot stand up by itself, yet it is more successful as a shrub than a climber. It flowers in summer, and is quite amusing, having blush flowers with a carmine stripe, and dozens of petals packed tight as can be.

The more peacefully inclined climbers are just right for growing on low walls or fences, or on pillars. I like pillars, and shall return to them in due course, for they are the exclamation marks of the garden. 'Allen Chandler' has large semi-double crimson flowers, mostly in summer, and 'Crimson Shower' is a restrained rambler which saves its flowers until late July and gives a most valuable contribution during August. 'Phyllis Bide' is good for late flower too, though the blooms are small. A very successful variety is 'Zephirine Drouhin', nearly a hundred years old, but as good as any for freedom, and fragrance. 'New Dawn' is a delightful blush rose, good as a pillar or a shrub. If you have a sunny wall, and can persuade 'William Allen Richardson' to grow, you will get considerable pleasure from him. 'Pink Perpétue' is also very fine, a pleasant shade of pink, and long in flower.

Group XII—up to the roof

Most climbers will grow quite a long way, and in the amount of wall that can be covered for a few shillings, they have the decorating industry beaten every time. Clg. 'Christine', Clg. 'Ena Harkness', Clg. 'Étoile de Hollande', Clg. 'Mrs Sam McGredy', all produce the well-known Hybrid Tea flowers on climbers. 'Danse du Feu' is a most striking scarlet variety, flowering summer and autumn. 'Guinée' is a wonderful crimson rose, unfortunately on a straggly plant. 'Meg' has some recurrent bloom, she is semi-double, apricot pink. But for sheer rose distinction in climbers, 'Mermaid' is hard to beat. Wide flowers, five petals only, cream at the petal, sulphur at the rounded ranks of stamens, pop into bloom here and there throughout the season. She is awkward as can be, brittle, breakable, with a wicked hook to her thorns. Hesitant to grow, she loses no time once she does start. She is one of the less hardy roses, and it is not unusual to find after a particularly cruel winter that an old 'Mermaid' has suddenly expired. She is worth all the trouble. 'Paul's Lemon Pillar', 'Parkdirektor Riggers', 'Mme Alfred Carrière', 'Mme Gregoire Staechelin', 'Leverkusen', 'Paul's Scarlet Climber', and 'Royal Gold' are all good. 'Sander's White Rambler' is a particularly pleasant rose, with a sweet scent. 'May Queen' is not often seen, it is a good pink with an old-fashioned look. 'Rose Marie Viaud', alias 'Amethyste', is an interesting mauve colour, and 'Felicité et Perpétue' is a rewarding white climber from Victorian days.

Group XIII—whither will you wander?

From 20 to 30ft (and very often much more), sounds a long way, but climbing roses can grow as far quite easily. Likely to find their length on those terms are 'Albertine', 'Chaplin's Pink Climber', Clg. 'Mme Butterfly', 'Emily Gray', 'Dr van Fleet', and 'Maigold'. The excellent 'Elegance' deserves special mention for its most delightful creamy-yellow colour in large and shapely blooms. So also does Clg. 'Cecile Brunner', the 'Sweetheart Rose' rampant, and a generous supplier of pink button-holes to all who pass by.

Conclusion

This survey shows us how varied is the material at our disposal. We have tried, in truth, to pick out from thousands of rose varieties and hundreds of different types, a representative few in 13 graded heights. The Rose List in this book describes those which to me are the most supremely beautiful, but there are many more which may appeal to you. We have not mined out the riches of the rose by any means. No one man can fully appreciate them all.

We should remember also that we can obtain roses budded on standard stems, usually at heights of $2\frac{1}{2}$ to $3\frac{1}{2}$ft, or at 5 to 6ft for weeping standards.

I hope this brisk look at the genus *Rosa* has been helpful. We have talked of what we saw as we passed by, but the journey has been only a preliminary reconnaissance. A closer look at the varieties will certainly convince us that some, however appealing at first sight, are not for us. In the Rose List I omit these, include others. There are some blank pages at the end of the Rose List, so that you can write in the names of roses which come out after this is written; for writing on the subject of rose varieties goes out of date as fast as the fashion columns in the *North Rutland Advertiser*.

Please remember that the heights are variable. By likening them to various parts of the anatomy, we have a rough and ready guide which ought to be a great help when planning the garden. But it may not always work out exactly so, and if anyone should become aggrieved in future, I shall have to search for either a pigmy or a giant to justify myself. The trouble is that I do not know in advance which of the two will be required.

3 Sounding the site

This chapter explores the loves and hates of the rose, thus enabling us to divide the garden into parts suited to roses and parts useless for them. From that point we shall then be able to plan the suited parts for roses and the useless parts for other things. Moreover, every gardener is under pressure from friends, relations and nurserymen to plant all sorts of odds and ends. This kindly blackmail should be resisted; but if from time to time we are obliged to accept Grandma's lily-of-the-valley or Aunt Bertha's belladonna, we can quietly plant them in those places which we have marked as useless for roses, and the probability is that they will fade away without any fuss.

As we begin to plan a rose garden, the first decision must be to plant roses where they will grow happily. It is an astounding fact that this clearly logical step is not taken by many a gardener. Where is the sense in drawing up a beautiful plan which claps the roses into a horticultural Dartmoor? What is the use of buying a dozen roses if next summer they look sad and sorry, plainly expressing their indignation at being barred from the sun? Our first step is observation, and it will pay us time and again, keeping us from wasting money and from failure and disappointment.

So let us look into the private life of the rose, and consider each factor essential to its well-being, remembering we have to supply all the things they love, not just some of them.

First love—sunshine

I suppose it is possible for roses to have too much sunshine, and indeed they are not entirely successful in the middle of the Sahara. But in this sceptred isle, seldom or never will too sunny a place be found.

Any part of the garden in full sun is a hopeful place for roses, and any part in complete shade is hopeless.

Between these extremes are places in partial shade, and there, somewhere, lies the dividing line we must learn to recognize. It is reasonably safe to assume that the dividing line between good and bad is the halfway mark.

Therefore a site shaded from the morning sun needs to enter

the sun's rays somewhere around noon. A site shaded from the afternoon sun should sunbathe till noon.

So many people have planted roses in defiance of this general rule, that there are plenty of exceptions to be found. Even in nature we may find wild roses growing in the woods, but it is rare to see them looking pleased with life.

Second love—comfort

If you have ever walked in ill-fitting shoes over five miles of loose desert, you begin to appreciate that comfort is an aid to physical efficiency in the human frame. Plants too carry out their daily duties far better if they are comfortable. The factors which we are now considering are wind and water.

Wind of itself is no enemy to a rose tree, apart from the breakage and rocking it causes. In testimony, consider the very open sites where wild roses grow. Nobody need fear wind, unless standards or climbers are insecurely tied, or unless the garden is at a site so exposed and notorious for furious wind as to interrupt plant growth. The only answer in that case is a wind-break by trees, hedges, or fencing; if trees or hedges, then sufficiently far away not to interfere with the third essential which is to follow. It is surprising how great a difference is made by wind-breaks, so noticeable in well-hedged fields, so beneficial to the plants thus protected.

The ordinary garden will not be troubled by wind, unless it is on top of a mountain, or perched with extensive views of the Atlantic. But many gardens have a species of wind which is unpleasant and uncomfortable. We shiver and complain when a draught blows through the room. Our plants feel just the same about draughts in the garden.

Where there is an opening into the property, there is a likely place for a draught. A gap in the hedge, a passageway between our house and next door, a gateway; these are the places to study. Where a continual current of cold air flows, plants will be unhappy. Draughts are a common cause of mildew, which to plants is rather like a cold to humans. A hot water bottle, aspirin and off to bed for us, and the cold is gone. But the poor plants remain out in the draught and their cold gets perpetually worse.

These places are not easy to recognize until the sufferers reveal them by their symptoms. But do keep an eye open for them. If on a fine day you cannot feel comfortable in the deck chair, you have found a suspect draught course.

Water can be a more serious problem. Given enough water we thrive, given too much we drown. As for us, so for plants. The chances are that your garden drains well, and you do not notice pools of water lying on the surface for long. Then all is well. But some people are not so lucky, they have either part or all of the garden lying under water for much of the winter. This is one of the most difficult handicaps to overcome. Good feeling prevents us from draining it off into the neighbour's garden. Probably the water table is high, and hopes of digging a mighty sump to soak the water away are frustrated by finding the sump unable to drain itself. The only hope remaining is to build up, to raise the beds and other planting places 12 to 24ins above the natural level of the ground. Better still, don't move into that house at all!

Third love—full board

In a few minutes a rose can be planted; and many a rose tree has looked up in anguish at its retreating owner, as much as to say 'there isn't thirty years' board and lodging here! I can't nip down to the grocer like you!'

We need a decent fertile soil for our roses. They will accept a very wide variety of soils, and are equally at home on heavy or light land, provided both are fertile. It is widely held that you need clay to grow roses, and people have actually imported this dreadful and intractable substance in subservience to that belief. Quite unnecessary! The truth is this: roses like to have their roots firm in the ground. On a heavy soil, once trodden in, the roots are firm —practically concreted in. On a light soil, they work loose. All they need is more boot—not clay at all—until they have taken hold. Therefore we need not mourn the absence of clay. If the garden is growing good strong plants, whether cultivated or just weeds, it will grow roses too.

Look out for places where the soil is not good; where the drain diggers have left subsoil on the top; where even the weeds are poorly, these patches are not for roses, unless we are prepared to do some soil shifting. Dig trial holes—see the depth of the top soil. If it is 9ins, no need to worry. If it is less, we can still grow roses, but must make a mental note to improve matters when we make the beds. If it is almost pure subsoil, chalk probably, as some gardens are, we shall have to import soil to have any reasonable hope of success. More of these matters in the chapter 'Making the beds'.

Everybody knows about the pH, I hope, for I have never really understood it myself. What it means is that roses like chalk in their soil, as I like sugar in my tea. Chalk is calcium carbonate ($CaCO_3$), known inaccurately as lime, and when it is present, it makes the soil alkaline, that is to say sweet; when chalk is absent, the soil may be acid, or sour. The degree of acidity or alkalinity is measured by the pH scale, and for roses we need, ideally, a pH reading between 5·6 and 7·2.

Observation and asking your neighbours will normally take the place of a soil analysis. If roses are flourishing all round, and the soil looks rich and deep, you will assume all is well. If roses are flourishing, but your soil contains a lot of chalk, you may safely assume you have a fairly high pH reading, and then you buy some peat, make it damp first (the easiest way is to let the rain do it) and dig it in. This will help reduce the alkalinity. You can be generous with the peat. It is cheaper by the bale, and is good for poor alkaline soil.

If on the other hand your neighbours' roses are weedy, and the district is full of rhododendrons, then you may suspect that you have an acid soil, needing chalk. Here must come a word of caution, because it is better to understand what chalk does before you start slinging it about.

Chalk, or rather calcium carbonate, releases carbon dioxide. This gas combines with the acids present in the soil in such a way that the acids release their bitterness into the air. The presence of those acids prevented soil bacteria from becoming active—but once the acids depart, the bacteria get down to work, and decompose organic matter. In doing so, they release plant foods into the soil.

It is thus obvious that calcium carbonate accelerates the decomposition of organic matter and in fact it is particularly quick to act on salts of ammonia. Therefore calcium carbonate is never applied with, or on to, farmyard manure, or compost, or sulphate of ammonia. It is better to put the chalk on first, a month before the others.

To add chalk to poor soil is unwise, because a poor soil is short of organic matter, and the chalk will therefore take away what little there is. Chalk cannot replace plant foods which were not there in the first place.

One must be cautious in the use of chalk, and I should myself need good evidence of acidity before I applied any. On a soil which is obviously acid, in rhododendron and heather growing districts, I should apply 2ozs to the square yard. On the strength of a soil analysis showing a pH reading of less than 5, I would apply 4ozs of calcium carbonate to the square yard.

To give your roses full board and lodging is the secret key turning the mediocre into the fantastic. The point we are making at present is that we need a reasonable soil.

How would you like to sit down to dinner, and find placed before you the plate emptied by your predecessor at table? Roses planted in old rose beds are treated so. If there are any old rose beds in your garden, they are the last place for new roses—unless you have the energy to change the soil.

'Full board', says the landlady, with a convincing smack of the lips. But suppose a dexterous individual at the neighbouring table helps himself from your dish as the waiter passes!

Many a rose tree would nod in sympathy; all too often a rose root is just about to inhale a delicate morsel, when whoosh! like underground Hoovers, tree roots and hedge roots sweep everything into their maw.

Trees and hedges greatly restrict the development of other deep-rooted plants within their trawling limits. You can reckon that the height of the tree is equal to the radius from its trunk within which roses will feel some ill effects, diminishing as the distance increases.

We can summarize this chapter in three first steps to make our plan.

1 *Sunshine* Note the areas good for roses
2 *Comfort* Cross out draughty and waterlogged places
3 *Full Board* Cross out places with bad soil, places where old roses are growing, places under the influence of trees and hedges

We now have a plan of the garden, either on paper, or on the ground or in our mind, showing where we have the optimum conditions for roses. We can go on to make the best use of it. But before we do so, a word about the areas dismissed from consideration.

In reserving the choicest areas for roses, we are left with garden space in which, if we are wise, we will grow plants to add character to the rose garden. We may also put there everything else the wife asks for. I will now add a little letter for you to read to her, because I like to be helpful, and I don't want you to be slaving away when you ought to be pottering among the roses. Pottering is very good for you. Slaving away is bad.

Dear Madam,

When planning a garden, you will appreciate that the time required in maintaining it must always be less than the time available. For this there are several good reasons, of which two will suffice: Two wet week-ends can ruin your husband's gardening schedule; a garden that once falls behind schedule becomes progressively worse, because all the work takes longer. Do make sure that your husband realizes this.

The most common mistake is to grow too many crops. You think of celery, strawberries, currants, raspberries, fresh vegetables, a rockery, fruit trees of course, and a herbaceous border (quite indispensable), some herbs, new potatoes, polyanthus, snowdrops, and don't forget some lilac. Also rhubarb of course. And delphiniums!

Lady, you are dreaming of the days when good gardeners were employed full time at thirty bob a week. The more different crops you have, the more work there is, because they all want attention, individual attention. If gardening is to be your number one spare time hobby, well and good. But is it?

Far better to lay the garden out so that it can be managed in swift bold strokes—straightforward sweeps—not in penny numbers. The answer is to ration your crops.

To give an extreme example, a perfect labour-saving garden can be made from four plants. *Grass*, the best foil for flowers, the best surface to play or to rest on. Fix yourself up with a good mower, make the lawn without too many awkward corners and edges, and it will not be hard to keep in order. *Daffodils*, most delightful of spring flowers; plant them and forget them. *Roses* (I believe your husband is taking an interest in these. He will tell you all about them. But there's nothing you would like better, surely?) and *Apple Trees*, which will give shade, flower in spring, fruit in autumn; plant them and forget them; you can prune them if you like, but they will still give fruit if you leave them alone.

With a garden like that, your husband will have more time to spend on YOU. Don't take that pleasure from him.

Yours very sincerely,

J.

(Note to husband: Those places you can't use for roses will come in handy for grass, daffodils and apple trees, perhaps a small conifer or two.)

4 Plan first

The poets speak with contradictory voices about planning. Rabbie Burns announced that 'the best laid schemes of mice and men gang aft a-gley' and we know exactly what he means without asking for a translation of 'a-gley'. Robert Browning, on the other hand, too optimistic to take Burns' word on the subject, had some faith in planning:

> 'Image the whole, then execute the parts—
>   Fancy the fabric
> Quite, ere you build, ere steel strike fire from quartz,
>   Ere mortar dab brick'.

There is no doubt that Browning's idealistic concept of planning is several lengths ahead of Rabbie's rueful one in popular favour at this moment. We are used to Town and Country planning, family planning, planning permission, five-year plans, and I don't know what else. If all the Britons who earn their keep by making plans, inspecting plans, passing plans, seeing plans adhered to, copying plans, filing plans away, attending planning committees: if all those Britons were to parade in single file on the main line from King's Cross, I daresay British Rail would need to extend the railway to the Shetlands to get them all in. And what better opportunity for them to do it, with all those planners to hand?

All the same, every now and then some plan goes sour, just like Rabbie Burns said.

I remember looking at a group of roses at Chelsea Show, probably about 1949. An elegant young lady was speaking to the nurseryman, and such was the press of people around that I could not avoid hearing the conversation. She was trying to make him plan her garden, and he obviously did not want to do it—no doubt for good business reasons. The way he got out of it amused me:

'Oh, Madam! Surely you want to have your own individual inspiration reflected in your rose garden? Think what it will mean to you in future years to say "I made this"! Far better than ordering one off the peg like everyone else.'

Planning is a matter of temperament. Some people take infinite pains to plan each detail. The result is successful in ratio to the soundness of their basic principles and their correct assessment of each detail.

Others like to live in a place without worrying about a plan until suddenly, one day, they see just what they want, and a flash of inspiration causes everything to fall in its right place. The basic principles must have been appreciated correctly if indeed all is to come out right. We will try to indicate the essential framework in this chapter.

The pathways

From our studies so far, we know where the roses can be grown, and consequently the garden should be planned around that basic fact. Day to day experience will teach us where to make our essential pathways, and it is just as well not to make them permanent until we have discovered the most pleasant walk to the front door, the back door, the garage and down the garden. While I do not like to go out of my way, I also like to see a curve in my pathways.

But the curve must be art for use's sake, not art for art's sake. A sensible idea is to use the garage entrance for cars and people, then your pathways can curve away from that common entrance to the necessary destinations quite naturally. Thus the garden, especially at the front, can be saved from the fate of being split into small rectangles, and your privacy may be more effectively secured.

Let us attend to the front garden, once the paths are settled. Assume the garage is to one side of the house, whether left or right, and from the garage gates a footpath curves gently to the front door. I should let it go across the garden, as being a more natural and direct route, keeping your visitors a little further away from the windows. 'Stepping stone' pathways can look very pleasing in grass, and pathways can be broken to admit pockets of thyme and other plants, provided the soil level ensures nobody will trip and break their neck.

The front hedge

Our primaeval instincts teach us to fortify our houses, but instead of digging moats and ramparts, we now plant hedges. In garden cities, and progressive places, it is felt to be more civilized to plant no hedge, but to leave the front garden and house open to the view. Some local authorities go so far as to prohibit hedges, or limit their height, an attitude a tenant may justly chafe at, for when authority enters one's garden gate, liberty lies down on the compost heap. Hedges are agreeable for birds to nest in, and to shut out the eyes of the curious. They may be dangerous to traffic, especially at street corners; and vehicles entering and backing out from a driveway which is closely guarded by tall hedges, may put at risk children on tricycles, or at play. They are a darned nuisance to keep trim.

The answer is to grow a rose hedge. If you want an open front garden, then plant a neat Floribunda hedge to grow 2 or 3ft high; be faithful to your purpose, and use only one variety for the hedge. The bed should be 3ft wide, and you will need one rose per foot run of the hedge. When planting, mark your first row with a line along the frontage, 6ins from the centre of the bed. Plant a rose every 2ft. Then mark the second row 6ins the other side of the centre, and plant a rose at every 2ft, in between the plants in the first row. Some of the best varieties for this purpose are 'Pink Parfait', 'Dandy Dick', 'Orangeade', 'Orange Sensation', 'Iceberg', 'Sir Galahad' and 'Escapade'.

Such a hedge will make a cheerful boundary mark, and yet leave your property open to view. But perhaps you prefer privacy? In that case we can erect some thorny palisades in several ways. The best is 'Queen Elizabeth', the pink rose of sturdy upstanding growth to 5ft or even more. For this you need a bed 3ft wide, and you can plant a single row along the centre of the bed, the plants 21ins apart. At this spacing, you need 12 plants per 21ft of frontage. 'Queen Elizabeth' is without doubt the ideal rose for this purpose, but others which may be used are 'Joseph's Coat' and 'Scarlet Queen Elizabeth'.

Climbing roses may be trained as fences of any height you choose, to make a hedge that few would care to penetrate. Unfortunately they are apt to wave thorny tentacles in the faces of passers by, and this could lead to unpleasantness.

Of the shrub roses, the Rugosas are the best hedge roses, dense, impenetrable, and well covered with foliage. Scabrosa is the best, but it will tend to grow fairly wide, and should be planted 3ft inside your boundary. A planting distance of 2½ft is suitable for this variety.

Do not be persuaded to plant a sweet briar hedge near a thoroughfare for it can be a danger to innocent pedestrians, for it grows in a manner similar to wild briar in hedgerows.

If you plant a rose hedge along your road frontage, buy the roses in the spring, and prune them before you plant them, by cutting the shoots down to the first eye, or about an inch high if you cannot see the eye. Then plant them without any labels on, for you know what the variety is in any case. These precautions may ensure that rose thieves walk by without noticing them. You will get a better hedge too.

The front garden

The front garden now consists of the paths and hedge, and the disposition of the remainder depends upon the aspect of the house. If it is facing north, we are probably limited to a simple area of grass and paving, with some gallant shrub or small tree placed where it looks pleasing. The lawn should be made just slightly higher than the paths, so that it can nestle close to them, and mowers can run from lawn to path without stubbing their blades on stone or concrete.

Any shrub or tree planted in a small garden should be one attaining moderate size at maturity; or else it should be cut down with resolution and replaced when it outgrows its site.

If the front garden receives sunshine, we have more scope to grow roses—and what is better than to be welcomed home by the scent and sight of roses at the door?

The obvious possibilities for growing roses in a sunny front garden are to screen off the drive and garage with a fence bearing climbers; to have a rose hedge between your neighbour and yourself, tall or short whether you desire privacy or communication; to have a bed by the house; and climbers on the house wall.

The lawn should be left as an unbroken pool of grass, so that it can be cut easily, preferably any shape but square. The pathway to the front door may cross the lawn, but it may be better still to lead it between the lawn and your roses.

No matter how you adapt these suggestions to your own use, it is better not to make too many beds.

If you choose to have a rose hedge between your neighbours and yourself, the instructions given for the 'front hedge' still hold good; with the addition that you can probably risk growing more spreading varieties without causing offence. Therefore we can add such varieties as 'Penelope', blush, growing up to 4ft; 'Nevada', single white, very spectacular, growing about 6ft; and 'China Town', yellow, growing about 5ft. These can be planted in a single row, 2½ft between the plants.

The idea of screening the drive and garage with climbers may not appeal to everyone, but it will certainly give a greater sense of enclosure, to say nothing of its beauty. Quite a cheap fence will do, consisting of some strong 7 or 8ft posts, preserved for longer life, and driven firmly into the ground. They may be joined with quite inexpensive material as the plants come to need support; a reel of old telephone cable is quite suitable. The posts should be 8 to 12ft apart.

Climbing Roses become large in time, and pruning can be awkward if they are planted too close initially. The less rampant varieties may be planted 6 to 8ft apart, the more vigorous about 12ft apart.

Most people would probably plant different varieties to increase the days of the year when the fence would bear flower. Some of the best, none of them too wild in growth, are 'Pink Perpétue', 'Parkdirektor Riggers' (scarlet), 'Zephirine Drouhin' (pink), 'Sander's White' and 'New Dawn' (blush). These may be planted 6 to 8ft apart. Do not tie them to your fence until the young growth appears in the summer; and as the young shoots appear, tie them in as much to the horizontal as you can to begin with, so far as they will naturally allow themselves to go. When your plant has sufficient shoots, they ought to be spread out in the general shape of a peacock's tail.

While we are thinking of climbers, we might consider what to do about the wall of the house. The first necessity is to have the means of support and training. For this, nothing is better than vine eyes in the wall, and if ever you have a house built, it is just as well to ask the builder to put them in at the time. In the absence of vine eyes, it is possible, though not so convenient, to use trellis; or firm stakes suspending strong cable.

Climbing Roses can be a delight on the wall of a house, but they can also be a handful. It is better not to use rampant varieties, unless you propose to hire a cat burglar or steeplejack to prune them. Be content with climbers growing less than 10ft high, among which are 'Pink Perpétue', 'Golden Showers', 'William Allen Richardson', and 'Zephirine Drouhin'. These should all carry flowers, instead of bare stems, at eye level.

Remember that roses need moisture, and the foot of a wall can be a dry place, especially if the eaves hang over. Therefore some moisture-retaining material ought to be dug into the position before planting. It may be well rotted manure, or peat. Do not tie the plant in until fresh growths appear. These should be fanned out on the wall, peacock's tail fashion.

The sunny front garden is now a bower of roses: we have them on four sides, counting the front hedge, the neighbour's hedge, the screen of climbers by the drive and climbers on the house. Our path curves to the front door, to one side of it a pool of grass, to the other—what? More grass, or a bed of roses? Such a bed would take the eye from the windows of the house, and to that extent offer privacy as well as beauty. It should balance the front hedge, by contradicting it in height. If the front hedge was chosen to be short, the house bed may be taller; if the front hedge be tall, then the house bed may be shorter. It could very well contain Hybrid Tea Roses in groups of five of a variety, planted 21 to 24ins apart according to their vigour.

Insert into the pool of grass one well-placed object, offset to balance the rose bed, solitary to attract the eye across green space. Choose what you like—a short growing, slim conifer, a sundial, urn or statue. This is the one impediment you have when mowing the grass.

The themes in such a front garden are tidiness, colour, simplicity, and ease of maintenance. I have tried to express the plan in such a way as to give not a blueprint, but elastic ideas.

The back garden

Most gardens fall into three general types, which are: the *utilitarian*, where the grass is squared off by flower beds, and then the peas and potatoes start; the *disguised*, where hedges and screens break it into small sections to hide the peas and potatoes; and the *landscaped*, where probably the peas and potatoes are not allowed in at all.

If you want to grow fruit and vegetables, most certainly you should, because it is a quite delightful occupation—provided you are prepared to give time to do it well. To plan your back garden, you need to decide what things you wish to grow, and to ration yourself to the number that time will allow. Unless you have some skill and experience in gardening, you will find that the simplest garden requires more time than you expected. Regular attention, timely attention is essential. It takes three times as long to cut the grass when you let it grow too high; let the weeds take control, and you are in trouble. There is much to be said for starting in the simplest and easiest way; you can always branch out into fresh adventures in the future, when you decide that gardening is so satisfying that you long for more of it.

The possible position for your back garden roses is determined by our observations in Chapter 3. As a general rule, and unless large trees are near, it will boil down to the fact that you can put them almost anywhere in a sunny back garden, or you need to keep them away from the house in a shady back garden.

In either case, what could be more pleasant than to step out of the house on to paving, with pinks and thyme, saxifrages and even miniature roses, growing from spaces provided? And the paving stepping straight to the grass, without an awkward bed to be by-passed? If there is a little narrow border between paving and house, it is here that I would plant mint and sage and rosemary, with any other herbs pleasant to housewives. The mint will find it difficult to spread, and all are handy for the kitchen.

Climbing roses may be grown on a sunny wall; and just to make the house melt into the garden, a paving stone may be omitted, and a good shrub rose planted there. For such a position the Rugosa rose known as Scabrosa would be ideal, for it has superb foliage, many days in flower, scent, and large red heps.

An irregular shaped lawn appeals to me far more than a square one. Grass should be as natural as a pond, finding its own level according to the surroundings. If there is a pretty view anywhere, either to a distant point, or else to a tree in the garden, let the grass run up to it, and let your borders sway gently, not too sharply, towards it. If there is no such view, we have to make one, and inside the garden a tree is almost essential to provide it. The simplest and most useful tree is, I believe, an apple, allowed to grow naturally.

Assume, then, that on our bare plot, we emerge from the house on to paving, then on to grass; we may plant an apple tree towards the left end of the garden, and then our lawn will go towards it. From the apple tree we will curve a border of roses towards the house. We can back the border with climbers, lead a path through it, a path that slants so that you do not see it from straight on. Behind the border may be placed our fruit and vegetable garden—or if we do not want one, another lawn with more roses.

Obviously the same plan can work to the right equally well.

Or we can plant our focal point in the centre, and run lawn each side of it, with inverted U-shaped borders of roses; and still we can preserve an area behind.

Or we can take the whole area for lawn, to make space for croquet or clock golf or cricket, pushing our flowers almost to the edges of the plot.

Back we come to the first point—what do we want in our garden? If the mind is firmly made up, the plan follows automatically.

The thing to avoid is many small beds, rose prisons, with hard labour for the owner. Use bold, large beds if you wish to break into the grass. Best of all, break the grass with no more than one large bed, and allow the borders around to invade it. Every family should enjoy games on the lawn; I well remember the poor suffering stretch of green we had at home. Six bare patches showed bowling and batting creases; in the centre, a seventh patch marked the kicking off spot. On 6 November, an eighth patch was liable to appear.

The back garden fences ask for a living wall of roses, and one could do no better than use Climbing and Rambler Roses. When they cover up the fences, they will provide a superb screen, giving privacy, and a sense of abundant space, because their effect is upwards as well as sideways. Imagine a child looking at a great Climbing Rose in full bloom. Even to us, it soars high—to the child, its rosy branches reach to the sky.

In your borders, let the Hybrid Teas and Floribundas be broken with good groups of Shrub Roses. Please have 'Canary Bird' somewhere, even if it is only one. The single yellow flowers, like large buttercups, are the most graceful intimation that summer is coming. A group of 'Nevada' and 'Frühlingsgold' will add height, character and beauty to the garden. Plant each variety in groups of five if you can. You can really see it then.

Much has been written on the virtues of mixed beds, as against beds of one variety. Where a hedging, or massed effect is required, use one variety only. That bold bed in the grass should be of one variety. In your borders, plant in groups, for it is interesting to see many varieties. To plant one of each sort shows you little.

When choosing varieties, always go for healthy, vigorous and free-flowering roses. Never be tempted by exotic and unusual colours, unless these three qualities are present. I write as a nurseryman, who wants his customers to be satisfied. Time and again we have tried to discard beautiful roses because they were frail, prone to disease, and shy in bloom; and yet people kept ordering them, to our confusion. You will be much happier with roses that give you no trouble. The list at the end of the book ought to help you.

Our back garden plan is vague, but the principles are there; and it is vague, because I sincerely trust that no two people will want to make their gardens alike. All I can do is to tell you the kind of garden I should enjoy, and leave you to tailor it according to your own wishes.

It is said that no garden is complete without water. I think this is true of a large garden; but in a small garden, and particularly if small children are around, water may be a mixed blessing. After all, we get plenty of it coming downwards in this country: it is one of those things you can always add at a later date, rather than as a first essential.

5 *Making the beds*

Two great commandments govern the preparation of ground. The first is that it shall contain ample food. The other is that it must be in good condition.

Food and condition are both requisite. Do not suppose that the one will suffice without the other. Any fool can fill the dog's dish with liver and let Rover go to sleep again; a sensible owner knows how to give his dog the right amount of food and exercise. What a difference there is between obese dogs, starved dogs and healthy dogs in good condition.

Plant food, then, must be applied sensibly, to ensure that fertility and sweetness will ensue in the soil. The soil must be so worked that it becomes friable.

The soil consists of myriads of particles, broken down over the ages from rock; and with these particles are the remains of vegetable and animal life, decomposed almost to their residual mineral contents, by the activity of countless organisms which live and increase in the soil. These organisms increase at a fantastic rate, when conditions let them, and in their living and dying the soil is continually and naturally replenished with plant food and with sponge-like material to absorb and hold water.

In nature, the soil particles are undisturbed, except by the roots of plants and the courses of insects, worms and water. The surface of the soil is regularly covered with fallen leaves and dying plants, the droppings and occasionally the dead bodies of all sorts of little creatures. Some of this surface mulch is taken underground by worms and insects; there, particularly if the animal residue has begun to work on the plant residue, the soil bacteria quickly form, and make plant food. What is left on the surface becomes a mulch, and some of its goodness is washed into the soil. This method of cultivation has been perfectly effective in constructing all the jungles and forests which once covered much of the earth.

When we seek to till the soil in order to grow plants of our own choosing, we are interfering with an intricate jig-saw puzzle, assembled by nature over many years. We need to put it together again as nearly right as may be. In fact we intend to improve it.

The first rule to abide by in operating on this remarkable

combination of a zoo and a chemical laboratory which we call the soil, is to let our operations be timely. Soil should be dug only when it breaks apart freely. Do not dig when the soil is so wet that it sticks to boot and tools; nor when it is too hard and dry.

Most soils can change from intractable to easy with a few days' weather. A dry day or two upon wet soil, or a wet day or two upon dry soil—and then, for perhaps only a limited period, your soil is ready to fall apart, and it is easy to dig. When the opportunity arises, one should act. Very often July and August may be splendid months for preparing the ground; once October arrives, the chance may be gone; but it returns in the spring.

Many people, on reading this, will say 'You ought to see my solid clay. It is never fit to dig.' But it is—unfortunately only for short periods. The best way to deal with it is to dig it piecemeal from July onwards, on the days when it can be broken. Then leave it lying rough over winter. Wait for the first drying days of spring, and you can do what you like with it. Miss the chance, and you will have lumps for another year.

Farmers and nurserymen are content to bide their time for ploughing until the conditions are right, and the soil loose to the boot. Then the tractors go to it without delay. It is accepted nursery practice not to tread on the soil when it is wet. That is the time when we do more harm than good.

Remembering the essential rule that our operations must be timely, done when the soil is ready for them, we may now set to work.

If the proposed bed or plot is covered with grass, let the turf be taken off, and put in a heap close by. Let a generous supply of plant food also be heaped close by, whether of animal manure, or compost, or just leaves, or peat mixed with a little bone meal; let it be bulky, and not in the form of any concentrated fertilizer whatever. Our aim is to supply material that will be converted into plant food, not the food itself. For if we throw in the food itself, our reasoning would be that of a man who realized that his car converted petrol into sparks, and therefore sought to fill his tank with fireworks.

We now dig out a trench across the end of the bed, about 18ins wide, and the soil is barrowed to the other end, where we shall finish. As we dig this trench out, we notice how deep our top soil is; and when we find that we are digging into the subsoil, whether white chalk, yellow clay, gravel or sand, then we stop, for we have no wish to mix this with the top soil.

At this point, we may have a problem, because if we have less than 9ins of top soil, the future outlook for our plants is not too bright. The sensible course is to take away a few inches of subsoil and replace them with so much good soil as to reach the minimum required depth of 9ins.

The trench is dug out, either to the subsoil, or to a depth of 12 to 18ins, according to your energy, resolution and ambition.

Now we leave that trench for a moment, and step back to the strip of soil which lies next to it. From this we take the top few inches (say 6ins) of the richest soil, and barrow it to the end of the bed. We have now, as it were, made two steps at the end of the bed, one dug 6ins deep, and the other 12 to 18ins deep.

Step into the first trench, and drive your fork into the ground, so as to break up the subsoil and create extra drainage and root run; but do not dig this subsoil up.

Now cast into the trench, roots upwards, as much turf as you removed from the top of it. Chop the turf with your spade. spread some manure over it, generously.

Your next trench has already had its top soil removed, so now dig the rest of it out to the same depth as you had dug the first one, spreading the soil evenly over the turf and manure in the first trench. As you do this, mix some more manure with it. Then step back to your third trench. Take the top soil from it, and spread it evenly, to complete the filling of the first trench.

Repeat this process, trench by trench, until you reach the end of the bed. There, the soil from your first trench, and the top soil from the second, will fill up the last two for you.

This is a thorough preparation, as is seemly for plants which are to enjoy board and lodging for many years. It is only fair to say that many people just plant their roses, and get away with it.

Having prepared ground in this way, the gardener ought to allow time for it to settle before he plants. We have upset nature's jig-saw puzzle, and she will slowly re-assemble it. The bed, when dug, is no doubt much higher than it was before. The reason is that it contains much air, in pockets between the lumps and pieces of soil. In due time, by the force of gravity, and by water carrying soil particles down, the jig-saw puzzle will interlock once more. Then those air pockets, so unpleasant to rose roots, will be reduced. If we plant before this settlement, it will occur after we have planted, and the soil we place so carefully around our roses will fall away, and leave the roots loose. They will not like that.

This is one reason why we advocate early preparation. Ground dug in July and August should be perfect for planting in October or November. Ground dug in September may be all right for planting in November. But if the ground is prepared in October or November, it would be better to plant in the spring.

6 On buying roses

The value of money has decreased so rapidly in this generation, that many thrifty people, previously advocates of investment, now openly state that the only safe treatment for money is to spend it quickly.

This deplorable, even immoral situation is the fruit of mismanaging our national household economy. Politicians should blush to see the present distrust of money accelerating its waste.

Every trade and profession, obliged to balance its books to stay in being, responds to the movements of money value. It is therefore to the point for me to explain the ways in which the rose trade has adapted itself to selling rose trees.

According to recent figures, it would seem that nearly 50 million rose trees are sold in Britain in a year. That makes practically one each for every soul in the country, or enough to fill 5000 acres of garden room.

Of these roses, approximately 30 million will be first quality plants, and 20 million smaller, whether of second or third quality.

The 20 million smaller trees are sold for the greater part, by advertisements in the papers, inviting mail orders; and for the lesser part, in suitable containers in stores and markets. They may usually be recognized by their price, which should be about one quarter to one half of that charged for a first quality tree.

The 30 million first quality trees are sold for the greater part through stores in suitable wrapping, and for the lesser part by people ordering direct from the nurseryman who produces them, either from press advertisements or catalogues.

There is some difference in the grading of roses as between one grower and another. The largest chain stores who market roses contract for the entire crops of their growers, and their stock will probably contain plants both of first and second quality. As the prices are usually very reasonable, a discerning purchaser may often find a good bargain.

Many shops sell pre-packed roses in polythene wrapping. As a general rule, the largest plants are difficult to wrap in this way, whereas the small ones are easy. The method of packing and distribution is costly, resulting in a price little different from what a producer charges for a direct order. If the price is low, so usually is the quality.

The best known names in British rose growing are those of the nurseries who are selling their own plants direct to the man in the garden. Such nurserymen are Wheatcroft, McGredy, Dickson, Harkness, Cocker, Gregory, Cant, Fryer, Mattock, Le Grice, and Lowe. These people, and many others, are staking their reputation on the quality of their trees. Their prices per single plant may be higher than prices in shops, but their prices for quantities will often be found cheaper.

Roses may also be bought growing in containers at garden centres. In my visits to these establishments, I have not invariably found a really good batch of trees. The reason is quite obvious. Roses are not particularly easy to maintain in good condition in containers; trees with large roots do not go into the containers readily, and who would pot a rose tree if he could sell it bare root? Therefore, many of the container grown roses are second quality being grown on. There are some garden centres with good quality roses, and I gladly omit them from this criticism; but as I have seen, so I have written. The prices are usually on the high side having regard to the quality. This is not surprising in view of the extra handling.

From the foregoing observations, I draw the following conclusions: buy direct from the producer if you want the highest quality in varieties of your own choosing; buy from stores, inspecting the plants carefully, if you want to save on the cost and are willing to take what varieties they have; buy the cheap roses advertised in the papers if you do not care about quality, and are prepared to wait a year for the plants to grow to a reasonable size— you may be lucky in quality with these offers occasionally. Buy from garden centres the odd plant to fill up a gap in the growing season.

It is only fair to point out that plants in stores often show signs of deterioration. From being dug up at the nursery to being picked off the counter, roses can wait for many days. The direct producer and the newspaper advertiser are both able to cut this time down, and thus avoid unsuitable shop storage conditions.

One would think the container grown plant in a garden centre would be the liveliest one to buy, but this is not my own experience. Container grown rose trees require to be planted with the soil damp right through, with all sides of the soil block firmly against the surrounding soil. This is not so easy to achieve as it sounds, and when it is not achieved, container grown plants have a nasty habit of standing still in dry weather, because the soil block and the surrounding soil tend to contract, and leave air pockets through which roots do not easily penetrate. You might think the answer is to plant when the soil block and the soil are both dry, and then soak them, but this does not work either, because the soil block allows water to run from it.

I must confess that as a producer of roses, selling them direct to the man in the garden, I am an interested party; but the evidence I have given is the truth to the best of my ability to tell it.

Having written much about the quality of rose trees, I should now endeavour to say how a tree is judged. This will help you to find that bargain in the stores.

The first requirement is that the tree should be in a fresh condition. Never buy, or accept a tree which is bone dry, or is showing signs of desiccation.

Secondly, it should be healthy, without any diseased foliage, or damage at the union where stems and roots meet. Such damage when bought may mean canker in a year or two.

As to size, we inspect three parts: the rootstock, the roots and the stems; and we take them in that order of importance. The rootstock is the part between the roots and the stems. It is the channel through which must flow all the materials that travel from roots to stems. We require it to be a good, wide channel. Take a finger thickness as a guide, and look with suspicion on rootstocks that are much thinner. The British Standards Institute says that the rootstock should be not less than 16 millimetres in diameter.

No tree is any good without plenty of roots. We want to see them running out freely; not twisted and cut short. The British Standards Institute standard for roses says there should be at least three major roots, running at least 10ins from the union; and there should be ample fibrous rootlets as well.

Most people judge a tree by the amount of wood on top of it. As this is scheduled to be pruned off, it is obvious that its length is of little importance. What matters vitally is the thickness and the ripeness of that wood.

The wood needs to be hard, so that it will not yield to the pressure of finger and thumb. A shoot you can squash will be axed by the frost. The thickness and numbers of the stems will vary with different varieties. A first quality tree should have at least two strong shoots; the normal trade practice is to shorten them to 12 to 15ins in the case of Bush Roses, and some nurseries will send them pruned ready for planting in the spring.

The trees to refuse are those with soft wood, disease, damage at the union where it cannot be cut away, thin rootstocks, small roots, and with such poor shoots that the sum of their diameter is less than the diameter of the rootstock.

Thus far we have surveyed the main selling methods, considered the product we are likely to get from each one, and described a good rose tree. I wish now to presume that we are going to buy direct from a nurseryman, since this is the trade I know best, and I would like to tell you a little more about it from the nurseryman's side of the fence.

Most people know nurseries through their catalogues. We in the nursery business are anxious to sell you the roses that will do well. But we have to sell roses to stay in business; and the publicity boys are telling us that unless we jazz up the catalogues, pitch a good yarn, tempt you with pictures of perfect roses (faked if necessary), throw in some pretty girls and urge you to do the Joneses in the eye; unless we do all these things, we shall not sell the roses.

Personally, I hate all that racket, and like to write my own catalogue as accurately and factually as I possibly can. I freely admit that the publicity boys are right, if the number of trees sold is the criterion. And many people enjoy the fun and exuberance of a make-believe world where all is right, everything perfect in prospect, where 'the greatest' glares at you from every frantic page. To be honest, it drives me up the wall. The plain truth is far more interesting, it requires a little more study, that is all.

From the above remarks, it will not be unreasonable to assume that the astute have resolved to take a pinch of salt with their rose catalogues. A little caution is needed in choosing your varieties. The plants you receive from any good retail grower should give you satisfaction. If not, just send them straight back. We would much rather be told of our mistakes, than have you dissatisfied.

When you receive good plants in good order, you should blame yourself if any fail to grow. Nevertheless, most nurserymen will replace the odd one that fails in its first year; and some make guarantees to this effect. But it is no use telling your nurseryman that none of them grew, because he will know you have done something silly to them.

It is not generally realized that nurserymen, like vine growers, have vintage years. We do not grow an identical crop of roses year after year. We expect to achieve a high standard, like the vintners, but some years are better than others. I believe that I could list all our own crops, going back to 1946, in order of merit.

It is often said that roses should be bought from a nursery to the north. Take no notice of this tale. It is based on the double fallacy that the climate is progressively colder as one travels north, and that roses grown in a colder climate will be more hardy. In actual fact, roses become hardy by making early growth, which becomes ripe in the sun, and is therefore hard wood by autumn. These conditions are dictated in part by cultivation, and in part by the soil and site of the nursery. These are essential points which the nurseryman ought to have assessed before entering his land. Roses can be grown tender or hardy within the same area, whether it be north, south, east or west.

When you wish to buy roses, think first what height you wish the varieties to be, then the colour and any other priorities you may have. Consult an impartial authority, such as the Royal National Rose Society's publications, or the Rose List in this book, where you can find colours and heights at a glance. This will give you a list of possibles—but who, but yourself, can tell if any of them is the rose for you? Therefore, you may wish to see the flowers, either at a rose show, or public garden, or at a nursery.

That is where the trouble starts, because after making a sensible choice, you are apt to be carried away by something else you found lovely on the particular day of your visit. The essential thing about a rose is to choose a long-lived, reasonably trouble-free variety. As a nurseryman, I have often tried to discard varieties which I knew to be nothing but a source of trouble, and having done so, I have been deluged by orders for that discarded variety. When people see a bit of colour, they forget about health, habit, vigour.

A sensible choice of variety can make so much difference to your garden, the difference between miserable bare beds and exuberant, healthy ones. So please be firm about it, do not be carried away by publicity, but choose for the appropriate height, for vigour, for abundance of flower and for health first of all. Colour, form and scent are the factors that sell roses easily, but to a discerning person, what use are these qualities unless on top of the right sort of plants?

7 Planting, the key to success

When your roses come into your possession, you have received living plants which need proper care and attention if they are to continue as such. It is a grave error to put away the package and forget about it for a week; if it contained livestock of the animal kingdom, immediate attention would be the order of the day. It is true that plants will not suffer so much nor die so quickly as animals; but they are livestock all the same; livestock of the vegetable kingdom.

If it is quite impossible to deal with them at once, owing to the inclemency of the weather or other emergency, they should be kept in those conditions which best preserve them. We know that they will live for months in cool storage, therefore they may be placed in a cool and draught-free shed. Most roses are wrapped in polythene, or polythene-coated paper sacks, for their journey to your door. The package should be opened, and the plants inspected to see that they are moist. If they appear dry, let them be watered and returned to the package. The mouth of the paper sack may be tied with string, and the plants can then be left for a few days in a cool place with safety. Should a long hard frost set in, it is likely that the shed will attain a cool store temperature, and thus safely hold the roses until the weather improves.

Notwithstanding those remarks, the right place for rose roots is in the ground. Again a difficulty may occur that the ground is not in good condition for planting, or the site insufficiently settled. Rather than botch the planting, it is advisable, and perfectly safe, to plant the roses temporarily. This temporary planting is known as 'heeling in', a bad descriptive name if it gives the impression that it can be done by shuffling one's feet in the soil; but a good description in the sense of the original Saxon word from which it stems, with the meaning of covering over.

The way to heel in roses is to dig out a trench about 12ins deep and wide. Dip the roots of the plants in water. Place the plants one by one against the side of the trench, with their roots sitting on the bottom; they may be as close together as you can conveniently place them, for a person skilled in placing them will probably get six plants side by side in a foot run of trench. Cover the roots with about 3ins of soil, and tread it firmly. Your plants ought to be sitting with the union where root and stems join below the level of the ground. Check that this is so, and if one is poking above ground level, put it down. See that the labels are above ground level, lest they should become indistinguishable after a few weeks' burial. Having checked on these points, put some more soil in the trench, tread it gently, and then fill up the trench to ground level. If you heel in rose trees like this, they can stand safely from October to March if need be.

When the day of planting arrives, let it be a day when the soil is in reasonable condition. If it is too wet for proper working, heel the roses in—not in the new rose bed, of course. Roses can be planted safely in frosty weather, provided the soil is not too wet under the frost, and if the frosty crust is put aside so that it may not be buried at the roots. Frozen ground, when buried, remains frozen long after the thaw.

Assuming that we can plant straight away, the order of work should be first to decide on the position for each plant. The roses should be left safely in their wrapping until the last moment.

The easiest way to mark planting positions is by using measuring sticks. The important positions to place are around those outside parts of the bed which will be viewed. Use one stick cut to the distance you intend to plant from the edge. This may usually be 12 to 18ins for bush roses, according both to vigour and whether you wish the roses to keep clear of a pathway, or grow over it. If in doubt, settle on 15ins. The second stick should be cut to the distance between the plants, usually 21 to 24ins.

Lay your 15ins stick on the ground with one end touching the verge of the bed, and at a right angle to the verge, as judged by a normally observant eye. Have sufficient canes or labels or any other convenient markers by you to enable you to mark the position of each plant. Place one of these markers in the bed at the end of your 15ins stick.

Now lay both your sticks down, the 21ins stick roughly parallel to the verge with one end against the marker; the 15ins stick again at a right angle to the verge, but about 21ins from its former position. Where the ends of the sticks touch is your next position for a marker. Continue right round the bed in this manner. You may have to lose or gain an inch on your positions to finish up with all equal.

The advantage of this simple method is that any bed, however awkward or irregular in shape, can be neatly marked out. For the positions towards the centre of the bed, you discard the 15ins verge stick, and substitute another cut to the length you require to separate your rows. It is probably better to stagger the rows, by planting the roses in the second row not straight behind those in the first row, but placed so that they come in between the planting positions of the first row. For a staggered row, the distance between rows can well be 18ins; for a bed planted in files, the distance should be 21 or 24ins.

When the bed is all marked out, and the inevitable adjustments concealed in the centre instead of glaring at us from the outside, let it be carefully observed from all future viewing sides for any faults.

In point of fact, this whole exercise could more wisely be done before the roses are ordered, for it is the only certain way of ascertaining the exact number required.

We are now ready to plant. The first question is where to start. The method of planting I am about to suggest is a particularly easy one, and it requires that the roots run to the direction of the sun. Determine, therefore, which side of the bed is facing in the direction of the maximum light. Go and stand on that side, and look at the bed. The place to start planting is on the far side from where you are standing.

Have ready spade, fork, secateurs, knife, a bucket of water and, if you so wish, a planting mixture of peat mixed with bone-meal. The latter is not essential if the beds were properly prepared, and is not altogether desirable if the ground is already acid and peaty; it is most useful if the ground is chalky.

Fetch out the roses, and cut away the package. Take the first plant, and put the packing material over the roots of the remainder. Put the roots of the plant in the bucket and move it around. Then, inspect the plant carefully, knife and secateurs to hand. Look first to the roots, which, being wet, will more easily reveal any suckers. The nursery ought to have cleaned these off, but you might as well make sure. Any little bump on the roots should be cut off with the knife. Any suckers which are not cut back completely ought to be whittled down level with the root. Any broken roots, or skinned root ends, should be trimmed off. Now examine the union, where smooth rootstock and thorny stems join. There may be a 'heel' here, where the original briar was headed back. If the nursery has left it sticking up, then you should cut it off, slantwise, just along the union and slanting down away from the union. Now look to the stems. Any leaves might just as well be picked off, for the sake of tidiness, although there is no objection to leaving them on. The plants will stand best about 12 to 15ins high for Bush Roses, 2 to 3½ft for Shrub Roses and Climbers. Cut them to this height, unless the nursery has done it already. You should now be holding a well rooted plant, with a sturdy rootstock, and two or three ripened shoots. Such a plant is ideal. Plants of different varieties are apt to be of different shapes, sizes and numbers of shoots. Having regard to these factors, if you think you have received a faulty or damaged plant, heel it in, and inform your supplier.

When the rose is planted, it will stand where the marker is, with its roots spread in an arc of 180° in front of the marker and towards the direction of the light.

To achieve this, stand with your back to the direction of maximum light, hold the spade with the front of the blade facing you, and the marker against the centre of the spade's back. Just nick the soil as a mark. You have seen the roots, and therefore can estimate the size of hole necessary. Nick out the rectangle accordingly. Now dig the soil out, only deep enough to accommodate the roots sitting down in it. Usually 6 to 9ins is sufficient. Do not dig the hole any deeper than necessary, or you will only disturb the soil, which is better settled. If you reveal any manure, just tread it down and cover it with soil. It is not good to let manure touch the roots.

Now sit your rose in the hole, with the rootstock against the marker. By setting the plant at a side of the hole in this manner, it is very easy to get the planting depth correct. The plant should be set with the union, that is where smooth roots and thorny stems meet, at ground level or an inch below. Put the plant there, and see how the roots sit in the hole, running more to the horizontal than straight down.

As a general rule, the 180° spread available to the roots will be sufficient. But occasionally you will have a plant with stiff, obstinate roots which cannot conveniently be so accommodated. If a root insists on going behind the marker, just make a nick with the spade to let it in.

It is usually agreeable to know the reasons for the things we do, especially in a case like this, when all our friends are liable to point out that roots grow straight down and ought to be so planted. Therefore we will pause here to examine the advantages of planting this way.

First, we have an easy way of judging the planting depth, for when a plant is put in the middle of a hole, and firmed in, all too often we find at the end it is too high or too low.

Secondly, by spreading the roots towards the horizontal, it will be very easy to attend to the most important part of planting a rose, namely to tread roots in firmly. We have a firm base to tread to, and this may not be so if we have the roots going downwards.

Thirdly, our roots are covering a considerable area. If we plant the roots growing downwards, and then tread them in, they will in the end have a lesser area to cover in their search for food and moisture than we are now giving them.

Fourthly, our roots are shallow; therefore, when the spring sun shines, they will feel its influence sooner than roots buried deeper, and growth will start sooner. It is not true that all roots grow downwards. Anchor roots grow down, feeding roots often grow up. We have made all our roots into feeding roots. The plant will seek anchorage quickly enough.

I hesitate to mention the fifth advantage, that we have a smaller hole to dig.

We have left our plant sitting in its hole, with its roots uncovered, while we considered these things. That of course was very wrong of us, so let us now cover those roots over with some fine soil (or planting mixture added to fine soil), 3 or 4ins of it, and tread very firmly.

While you are treading the roots in, may I encourage you with another digression? It is most important to plant roses firmly, and I would like to explain why.

Imagine a wild rose growing in nature, in soil which has not been disturbed by man. That soil is packed tight, since all the particles have tended to settle close together over the ages, guided downwards by the force of gravity and the courses of water. If ever you have subscribed to the operations of digging out hedges, tree roots, or drains, you will know how tight soil can pack itself. The tender rootlet of the wild rose, this delicate tendril of vegetation, slimmer than a hair, now forces its way into the block of soil around it. Already it is in close contact with the soil. As it grows, its girth increases, an occurrence not unknown to mankind. If when hair thin it was in close contact with the soil, then expanding it must press against the soil around it.

Thus, in nature, rose roots live in conditions of soil pressure. They have to, because they absorb moisture from the soil through pores on the root skin. If the pores are surrounded by air, they cannot absorb moisture sufficiently. They need soil close to them. That is why we tread the soil very firmly indeed when we plant roses. It is the essential factor in planting.

Having trodden the roots in firmly, we half fill the remainder of the hole, tread again, and then fill up to ground level, leaving the top part untrodden.

It should be possible to tug the newly planted rose sharply and feel it resisting, rock steady.

May I repeat the cardinal principles?—Plant firmly, do not bury the union too much, and let no manure or fertilizer touch the roots.

The time to plant roses is when the ground is right to receive them, which you may test by seeing whether it may be dug easily. Although tradition says that November is the best month, experience replies that roses planted in good conditions in April will grow better than roses planted in bad conditions in November. The answer is to heel them in and grab the opportunity when it comes.

October and November may be very pleasant months in which to plant roses. The soil retains some warmth, and rootlets are soon formed, truly cementing the plant to its new surroundings. When the soil is cold, in December and January, one may plant roses safely, but it is unlikely that rootlets will be formed. The plants are really being kept in the ground in cold storage. February may ally itself to January in some years, to March in others. But as the soil warms again, in March and April, so roses will quickly take root hold.

It is well, when the ground is dry in the spring, to tread round all your newly planted roses again, to make sure they are firm. This will be more necessary for those planted in the spring, when the soil may contract by drying quickly. If you see a plant failing to grow when the others have started, tread very firmly to tighten the soil round the roots. Then give it a bucket of water, to flood fine soil particles to the roots. This first aid is usually effective.

We can now see why people say you need clay to grow roses. In clay soils firm planting is easy—the stuff sets right round the roots. Roses will grow just as well in light soils, provided their owners achieve soil firmness at the roots.

Pruning is very good for the gardener's ego, for he becomes a kind of surgeon, operating on his plants to their benefit. Pruning is easy when the principles are understood, and the non-essentials relegated to their proper place.

The reasons for pruning have been brilliantly expounded by rose growers of a previous generation, and may be summarized as follows:

A rose is neither a plant like an oak tree, which through one main trunk channels sap to all its parts for several hundred years; nor is it like a delphinium, whose shoots do duty for one brief summer and die down again. A rose is in between the oak and the delphinium, using its shoots for several years, after which it gradually starves out the old shoots, and favours new ones. This is done because a rose shoot is capable of limited girth, not thickening year by year with added rings like a tree; therefore, when the limit of its natural girth is attained, it makes no more new, sap-conducting cells; and the older cells become yearly more woody and less able to conduct sap. As this stage is reached, the rose puts its energies into younger shoots, allowing the old ones to starve out and eventually die; and the younger shoots will in turn experience a similar life cycle.

For a vivid illustration of this occurrence, one need only take a walk down the nearest briar hedge. There may be seen great portions of the plants borne on old wood, and in process of starvation, their side shoots more like match sticks than rose shoots in size. Through and around these old parts, young thick green shoots will be thrusting. If one could see the bush in flower during the summer, it would be found that the flowers on the older portions of the plant were considerably smaller than those on the new. While this old wood remains with its tangled mass of years of top growth, it is restricting the full development of the younger shoots. In nature this does not matter, because seeds are produced all the same. But in our gardens it is very necessary to encourage the production of young and healthy wood with flowers of a proper size. Therefore we prune our roses so that the unproductive parts are cleared away, and prevented from hindering the full development of the productive parts.

From these reasons, it can at once be seen that there is one great key, and only one, which we need to unlock the mysteries of pruning. That key is the ability to recognize productive shoots, and I shall now endeavour to place it securely in your hand.

A productive shoot is ripe, stored with plant food, and not yet at the stage where its offshoots are weak and feeble. I often think that the rose tree welcomes you at pruning time, anticipating benefit as we do from the barber for our comfort and tidiness; and as we may ask for short back and sides and some off the top, so the rose tree extends its shoots, and short of speech it sits there fairly begging you which to cut off and which to leave on.

We know that productive shoots must be ripe, and this is so with all old wood obviously, as also with the young wood which grew soon enough last summer to ripen. But you may have some thick young shoots of late development last year which are soft and pithy. You will soon learn to recognize them, and the way to learn is by making some trial cuts in the upper part. A ripe shoot is firm, cuts crisply; an unripe shoot has soft pith, which crumbles slightly at the cut edge; a ripe shoot is hard, does not give way when pressed firmly between finger and thumb; an unripe shoot will give way, and suffer indentation from such pressure.

Next, productive shoots need to be stored with plant food. This is purely a matter of cubic capacity. Until somebody proves to me that a thick shoot contains less food than a thin one, I shall continue to believe the obvious, namely that ripe and thick shoots are likely to be more productive than ripe and thin ones.

Finally, when we come to inspect the older parts of the plant, we look to see if they are doing as they should. The older parts are, of course, the shoots we judged productive when we pruned the roses last year, and the years before. Perhaps some of them have few if any offshoots worthwhile—they will be considered unproductive, while those on which there is vigorous young side growth will be retained for another year.

If we look at a plant in this way, and ask it where it has stored its food and strength for future growth, an answer is reflected in the branches before us, and having understood we can proceed to prune.

Before we start cutting, let us just clear away one or two points of general interest. First, the tools; pruning roses with blunt secateurs is the sort of job the devil no doubt has in mind for sinful rosarians, should any happen his way. It is a joy to prune with good sharp tools, and the most pleasant ones that I have used are Felco secateurs. Keep them for pruning, and, when they get old, use them for other jobs and buy a new pair for pruning.

The time for pruning excites much argument; and it seems to me that as long as the plant is reasonably dormant, you can just choose a pleasant day without worrying what the calendar says. But I do not like pruning plants when they are growing, neither climbers in August nor bushes in April.

Give me a pleasant day in January, February, or March, for the job; and if no pleasant days come, or we missed them, and the roses begin to make leaf, then we have left it later than desirable, and ought to get out on the job as fast as possible. For when leaves appear on unpruned plants, valuable sap is feeding parts of the plant we do not need, and that much of the summer splendour is going to waste.

It is now necessary to take two separate ways in this chapter, for the method and reasons for pruning new plants and old are slightly different, as you will see.

Pruning new rose plants A new rose bush from the nursery may have sufficient eyes upon it to make thirty shoots. Meanwhile, under the ground, it has a root which will not start into effective production until the spring sun warms up the ground.

I am not enough of a botanist to know which comes first, the demand or the supply; or in other words, do the leaves grow first, and set the root machinery turning, or do the roots pump up food and make the leaves grow? We have grown plants in sand to find out, and some of them start root growth without leaves, and others leaves before root growth. On balance it seems to me that the roots lead by a short head, but to seek fresh anchorage rather than food; and the leaves promptly start the season's awakening by growing from food already in the plant, thus setting up a demand which the roots respond to.

Now if thirty shoots start growing on a newly planted rose, each with five leaflets, it is not long before 150 leaflets are making their wants felt; and the shoots need not go far before the number goes to 300, then 450, then 600. The unfortunate roots are starting from scratch in a strange position, as planted by some well meaning human, and certainly not in so advantageous a state as if they had the previous year to grow where they would. Therefore it will not be long before they protest at the demands of this large family of leaves.

When the roots prove unable to support the aerial growth, the atter will stop dead, and the proud owner will see precisely thirty tiny blind shoots. The plant will stand still, and start again later. Time and sap will have been wasted. In order to prevent this, we prune newly planted roses so that they may produce only so many shoots as they may reasonably be expected to support.

In the case of Bush Roses, we cut them down so that the length of shoot remaining is 2 or 3ins. It looks murderous, but do not be afraid. If your new bushes are pruned so that all that is left sticks out of the ground about a finger length, you have done right.

In the case of Shrub Roses, we leave them about 6ins long, and in the case of Climbers, about 18ins; in the case of Standard Roses, we cut the heads back so that finger lengths of the grafted part are left extending from the budded unions.

Those are the reasons, and the essential things to do. There are also two desirable non-essentials. First, any very short twiggy growths are cut away right to the base they spring from; and second (here comes the heresy) we do not lose a lot of sleep looking for an eye to cut to. If an eye is obvious, we cut just above it; but if an eye is not obvious, we cut to the height we want. In a few weeks the plant will be growing, and if any stub of dead wood is left above the shoots, we can take it out, if time permits, to prevent insects nesting in it.

Pruning old rose plants After the first year, conditions have changed in one important respect; the roots are now able to support all the top growth the plant cares to make; they are no longer in strange territory, no longer starting from scratch; and we no longer need to restrict the number of shoots our roses may carry.

One important consideration must however be remembered, and more particularly in the early years of the plant's life. It is more natural for roses to grow first from the eyes near the top of the stem. If we leave the stems long, we shall find as a general rule, though not invariably, that the top eyes will grow, and the lower ones may not. This is fine for a year or two, but then the day comes when at the base of the plant we have nothing but old wood, reluctant, through age, to make new shoots. Our plants have become prematurely aged because we did not cut them down low enough in their youth. The ideal situation is to ensure that some young wood is cut down low each year, and as the plant grows in vigour, so we can leave some shoots fairly long also.

It is necessary to subdivide this chapter a little more, because various types of roses require slightly different attention.

Bushes Look first at your bush, and ask it to show you its productive shoots.

These, as already stated, are ripe, thick, and capable of bearing growth. They may come from the base of the plant, or from some of the wood that was kept last year. Note carefully which they are. With practice, this can be done at a glance. The more difficult to assess are those coming from the older wood. It is likely that in any section of older wood, productive shoots may arise from any point upon it, whether near the base or the top. Observe the highest point upon the old wood whence a productive shoot rises, and resolve to keep the whole of the old system up to and including that highest productive shoot.

Having absorbed what the plant has to say about its productive shoots, we take the secateurs and cut out all the unproductive shoots. If unproductive shoots come from the base of the plant, we cut them back as close as we can to the base. If they come from old wood, which has no productive shoots on it at all, we cut the entire old shoot, with unproductive branches on it, down close to the base of the plant. If they come from old wood which has one or more productive shoots on it, we cut the unproductive ones back close to the main shoot from which they spring. And any of the old wood which extends beyond the junction with its highest productive off-shoot, is cut off immediately above that junction.

When this is done, we have left on the bush only the productive shoots, to their full length. The question now arises, how short to cut them?

The answer is, be firm and hard while the plant is young, and cut most of them down so as to leave 2 to 6ins on the plant. Cut the thinner ones down to 2ins, leave the thicker ones to 6ins. When your plants are older, and if you want them to grow taller, then you may leave your thicker shoots up as long as they are thick and strong—but only one or two of them, because you must keep some young wood growing near the base. If ever you prune a bush like this, it will look rather odd in April and early May, because you will have leaves near the ground, then bare stem, then leaves near the top. But once the gap is filled by the lower growth pushing up, you will have a very large and handsome plant for the rest of the summer.

Do not be afraid, especially when your plants are young, to be so ruthless in assessing productive shoots that you resolve to keep only one or two. From these a glorious plant can grow.

The most difficult plants to prune are those where you can find no satisfactorily productive shoots at all. Prune everything hard, and if the plant does not grow better next year, give your nurseryman a treat by ordering a new one.

If you see an eye, cut immediately above it. If you cannot see an eye, cut to the right height. The dead stub can be taken out after growth has started.

The more expert rose books are careful to tell you to cut to an outward facing eye, and no doubt this is sound theory. But in practice we find that roses do not necessarily make their subsequent productive shoots from the eye you cut to. More likely it is the second or third eye which makes the strongest shoot by the end of the summer. Therefore it is not necessary to worry about this sound theory. Cut to the height you want, above an eye if you can see it, but whether the eye faces inward or outward is not very important.

When you cut to an eye, or when you take out dead stubs after growth has started, it is well to make a slanting cut with the higher side of the slant next to the eye, or the young shoot as the case may be. The eye cannot draw sap horizontally through the stem, and therefore the line of dying back above the highest point of sap use is not a horizontal one, but a slanting one, sloping down from the eye-side of the shoot.

Shrubs There are two kinds of rose shrubs as far as we are concerned, those which flower on new wood, and those which flower on side shoots made from the wood of former years. The Rose List at the end of the book makes a point of saying which flower from the old wood. If we prune those back every year, we should obviously be defeating our object, because they are not going to flower from old wood which we pruned off and put on the bonfire.

The best way to prune such shrubs, is to cut them down when new, as stated under the heading **Pruning new rose plants** (p. 55). Then let them grow without being pruned at all, except to keep them within bounds, for three years. Every third year, inspect the plant, and recognize which parts of it are becoming old and unproductive. This you may tell by the strength of the side shoots made in the previous year. These sections should be sawn out at the base, or occasionally higher up if a productive part is originating from some point upon them. Do not shorten the long young shoots of these Shrub Roses, or you may spoil the pretty arching habit they have.

Many Shrub Roses flower in much the same way as ordinary Bush Roses, but on a larger plant. These may be detected in the

Rose List by the absence of any comment about their flowers being carried on side shoots from wood of former years; the difference is that the type of Shrub Roses we dealt with in the last few paragraphs devote a year, as it were, to launching a platform for next year's flowers. Therefore if we cut the platform away, we cut the flowers away too. But the Shrub Roses which flower as bushes are quite a different matter.

The Shrub Roses which grow flower-bearing stems in their first season, like bushes, should be pruned just like Bush Roses, except that you may leave the productive shoots two or three times as long; that is 6 to 18ins, according to the strength of the shoots. If you choose to keep some productive old wood, then even the weak side shoots on it can give you flowers again next season; cut the young side shoots back so that they are an inch or two long from their junction with the old wood.

Climbers Climbers take more time to prune than other roses, but they are interesting and satisfying to work on, and the principles remain exactly the same. Again, it is a matter of studying the plant to find its productive shoots, but the study is complicated by the greater size of the plant, and the more intricate tangling of the shoots.

I find that the easiest way to prune a climber is to start at the bottom of the plant, and to deal with one shoot after another, until the whole is done. We may expect to find three kinds of shoots, namely young ones without side shoots, two-year-olds with young side shoots, and three- (or more) year-olds bearing more complicated side shoots.

The young ones are easy to deal with. Provided they conform to our specification for a productive shoot, being ripe and thick, we retain them for their whole length; or if they are too long for the position in which they must fit, we trim off the end to measure.

The two-year-olds require a little more study. Working from the base of the plant, we trace them upwards, resolving that where they cease to satisfy us as to their value as productive shoots, there they shall end with a cut from the secateurs. Up to that point, we cut all the normal side shoots, so that when cut, they are protruding 1 to 2ins from the main shoot from which they spring. I say 'the normal side shoots' because there may also be some abnormal ones, growing a yard or more long, instead of a foot, which is normal. These long ones may, if the position can accommodate them, be treated as young shoots; and their full length, or the productive part of it, retained.

The three-year (or more) shoots should have had their side shoots pruned back last year, and from the inch or two that was left then, one or two flowering shoots may have grown. The strongest of these will indicate whether the old shoot is still worth keeping. Follow it up from the base of the plant, and if it looks productive, keep on pruning so that the new wood is about an inch long. On these shoots you will then have wood of various ages. The shoot itself dating from year 1; its first side shoots, cut back to 1 or 2ins, dating from year 2; and its further side shoots, which you are now leaving an inch long, from year 3.

Sooner or later, some of this old wood will plainly appear unproductive, and you may wish to cut the shoot out. If it appears unproductive for its entire length, it will come out at the base of the plant. More usually, you will find that at some point it branches out in a strong side shoot, and above this juncture there may be a very noticeable narrowing of the main shoot.

Such a point is an obvious boundary mark to the productive limit of the shoot. It should therefore be cut off immediately above such a junction, the strong side shoot being retained.

Climbers may well be pruned in the autumn, because after pruning they can be tied in, and the winds of the winter will not then harm them.

Right from the start of its life, you should tie the new shoots of a Climber out to the horizontal as much as possible. This will do two things. First, it will cover your support effectively, and secondly, if the shoots are to the horizontal, the eyes will tend to break into growth along the length of the shoot much more freely than if that shoot were upright.

If you are growing Climbers as pillars, the pruning remains the same in principle. A pillar is very easy to manage, provided you prune it annually. Cut loose the ties, prune the shoots one by one, as already explained; gather the plant up to the post, and tie it in. If it is obviously too tall for the post, either cut it off a foot above, or else buy a longer post.

Standards From what we said about the oak tree and the rose, it will be appreciated that a Standard Rose is not a natural thing at all. For in growing a rose on top of a single stem, the gardener is compelling it to spend its life in dependence on the sap flow through one channel. We have noted that it is natural to the rose to alter its channels of sap flow every few years.

Therefore a Standard Rose should not be expected to show

that vitality in producing new wood which is found in Bushes, Shrubs and Climbers.

After the first year, when a Standard is pruned hard, it will not enjoy hard pruning year after year. It will not be able to find new wood year after year. It will mature with a short and stubby head.

The way to prune a Standard is to imagine that when it is pruned, the plant will be the skeleton which in summer will be clad with leaves and flowers. So far as its development allows, keep the outline of the lovely plant you hope to see, and trust in it to persevere in growing through its old wood. If the outline is not there, you have no alternative but to keep in the best shoots, trim out the weak, and hope that it will fill the gaps another season.

9 Doctoring

If only we could grow roses without diseases, the greatest impediment to their enjoyment would be removed, and practically every garden would be full of them. But nature has a tolerant, catholic view of plant life. Roses, to her, are only one of the million and one living organisms which she conducts in her World Symphony.

Mildew is one of nature's favourite plants. It is a fungus, too lazy to take its nourishment from the soil like any decent plant; it chooses to let the roses manufacture food in their leaves, and then by growing on the rose leaves, steals supplies the rose has stored. Everyone can recognize mildew; it is a grey-white mould, often first appearing on the seed pod, and very obvious on the young leaves of roses. Mildew to roses is much like a cold to us. A strong and healthy plant may well outgrow mildew. A weak plant will suffer more. Nearly everything written in this book is designed to let your roses grow so strong that they do not succumb to diseases; and the prime reason why roses catch mildew is some interruption of growth.

Such an interruption will occur if the plants are in the wrong site; either too shady, robbed by tree roots, or sitting in a cold draught. Badly prepared beds invite mildew, for a plant which suddenly finds air round its roots, due to late soil subsidence, will stop growing and get mildew. Some roses, by faults in their constitution, can be guaranteed to get mildew. These I kept out of the Rose List in this book, unless they had some claim so particular as to demand their inclusion; in which case they are plainly marked 'mildew likely'; thus a person in the Black Country may enjoy them, for a sulphur-laden atmosphere prevents mildew. But if you already have mildew, try some other variety.

Mildew, although annoying and disfiguring, is not very serious. Blackspot is rather worse. *Blackspot* is a disagreeable fungus, so greedy that not content with stealing the food from a rose leaf, it also causes the leaf to fall. If this happens in high summer, the plant is robbed of those foods which the leaf itself manufactures, and its shoots may fail to ripen well enough to stand the winter.

Happily, blackspot requires conditions of temperature and

moisture which are not normally present in these blessed islands until fairly late in summer. When it does thrive, it produces spores at an alarming rate. For productivity it leaves modern industry far behind. A bed of roses suffering from blackspot is producing spores at the rate of millions per day.

Rose leaves are apt to become marked with all kinds of spots, and many people, on seeing perfectly innocent marks, imagine they have blackspot. The disease is most obvious by the large size of the spot; it is black, a circle with not a closed but a radiating circumference. It is large, up to the size of the head of a drawing pin. Again, our Rose List has omitted the worst varieties, and warned about those too beautiful to leave out on account of some liability to blackspot. In certain parts of the country, it is rarely seen.

The third fungus disease is *rust*. This is the most insidious of the three, for it penetrates further into the tissue of the plant. Rust may be seen early on by small floury marks on the underneath side of the leaves. These soon grow into clusters of little orange-coloured pustules. At this stage they are wafting spores through the air; in order to keep in good fettle through the winter, they put on their winter coats, by turning black.

The Rose List does not give a thorough guide to rust, for the simple reason that this disease has of late years been commoner to south-west England than to the rest of the country. Consequently, my knowledge of how varieties resist rust is not very great. But I have mentioned it in a few cases I know of, and some roses have been left out of the Rose List because of reports I have heard.

These are the three main enemies, and fortunately they can all be kept within bounds by the use of sprays.

Now it is my opinion that spraying is no fun, and it is very rarely that I ever spray my own roses. If a rose is prone to disease, I prefer to dig it out and plant another. But sometimes diseases need to be nipped in the bud, and as the materials exist, it would be folly not to make use of them.

The manufacturers of sprays often advocate that their materials be generously squirted over the garden to prevent any diseases from arriving. This, no doubt, is very sensible. But are you the sort of person who wants to spend money and sweat in preventing something that might not have happened anyway? I must confess I am not. If I see mildew, blackspot or rust early in the season on any variety, I will spray to stop the disease from spreading. If I do not see them until September, I do not worry. I think the plant is safe in September. But I should remember seeing blackspot in September, and I would spray the plants in the spring, as soon as I pruned them, to deter any spores staying for the winter.

Rust can be cleaned up very efficiently by Maneb. Where rust appeared last season, Maneb should appear in March. As soon as the plants are pruned, spray plants and soil; repeat within fourteen days, because some spore development may occur in this time. The double dose ought to slaughter your rust. There is no need to use any more Maneb unless rust appears during the summer. Then any infected plant may be sprayed, again twice, the second application within fourteen days of the first one. As rust grows on the undersides of the leaf, that is the essential side to cover. You need a decent sprayer for the job.

Maneb does blackspot no particular good either, and a similar programme may be followed to deal with that disease. I have not used Maneb myself, but have seen its effects in a garden in which I have a particular interest, and there it has been most efficient. Orthocide (Captan) is widely used for blackspot, and I am informed that a new material named Delancol appears to be good too.

The best spray for mildew seems to be Dinocap. In this case the spray can safely wait until mildew appears; prompt action, before it spreads, can wash mildew away quite fast. Karathane is also effective.

Many insects are fond of roses, but they can be dealt with by applying Toprose systemic on to the soil when it is moist, twice within ten days. Alternatively they may be rubbed off by hand when they are observed.

Whatever spraying you do, please follow the instructions most carefully. Do not spray on a sunny day; if your diseases appear in a heat wave, you may chance spraying in the evening. But a dull day is always preferable, to avoid damage to the foliage by the sun evaporating the moisture, and leaving an undiluted deposit on the leaves.

The secret of spraying is to obtain one hundred per cent coverage. Having read the instructions, and mixed the spray, many people fail to apply the stuff properly. The solutions recommended are within a good safety margin, and no harm will be done if you spray some of the plant two or three times. Unless you attain one hundred per cent coverage, a group of fungi will survive your onslaught, come through it unscathed, and continue to propagate their kind at a million a day.

I hope you do not need to do much spraying. Your choice of varieties will play a big part in whether you spray much or little. You have a good chance of growing roses without ever spraying them, unless you live in a district where disease is rife.

10 Care and attention

Our story is running near to its conclusion. Survey—plan—prepare—buy—plant—prune—doctor; these are the simple steps to enjoying roses. In this chapter I must mention the other few things which ought to be done.

Suckers When you see a sucker, take it out. It will be harder tomorrow.

Suckers grow from the plant which provided the roots of the rose; and in the case of Standards, the stem also. For these purposes wild roses are used, very often the dog rose, which by reason of its hardiness, and by being native to our country is well adapted to nurse roses budded on to it.

A persistent belief exists that nature has given roses five leaflets to a leaf and suckers seven. This is wrong. Nature does nothing of the sort. She lets both of them have five and seven and sometimes more on the same plant, even the same stem. The only ways to recognize suckers are by their appearance and their point of origin. Of these, the point of origin is the more certain. A sucker cannot grow from the rose itself. It must originate from the rootstock. Conversely, a budded or grafted rose can grow only from the budded union. It cannot suddenly jump to an entirely different place on the roots; only a rose grown from a cutting or from seed can do that, and apart from Miniatures, very few are grown in those ways commercially.

The chapter on planting contains information on suckers, and of this I wish to reiterate how essential it is to take out a sucker entirely. Leave a portion, however small, and it will respond gratefully to hard pruning, and grow with vigour.

Suckers which grow near the top of the bush can easily be removed, because they can be got at. Sometimes a sucker will come through the ground at some distance from the bush. Most likely this is growing from a surface root, and a gentle pull will prove the case. If it comes readily, root attached, cut through the root, and tread it back. If it does not come easily, then it is attached to a root better left undisturbed. Explore with a small hoe, or trowel, until you find the root. Cut through it on the plant side of the sucker, and pull out the sucker with the rest of the root.

No harm is done, for you have not disturbed the root, only pruned it.

The most difficult suckers are those which grow down among the roots, close to the plant. The best way to be rid of them is to pull them out, a highly unorthodox proceeding horticulturally. This may only succeed if the sucker is young. Let it become woody, and it will break easily, in fact you will be at risk of pulling up sucker, plant and all. But if it is young it may usually be torn away from its point of origin, with a small piece of root attached, and then it is well and truly disposed of. But for heaven's sake stop pulling if you feel the root below beginning to move. Delicate excavation must then be resorted to.

Old flowers Many people find that 'dead-heading' is one of the most pleasant tasks in the rose garden. You certainly get well acquainted with your roses by moving through them, removing old flowers.

The idea behind this practice is simple and sound. Once the plant can set seed, its purpose in life is achieved. Seed absorbs many nutrients. Therefore we remove the old flowers before they set seed, saving the nutrients, and obliging the plant to hurry up with some more flowers in order to perform its annual task.

Some people believe in carrying out this task as though conducting summer pruning. They claim that the next flowers must be produced on shoots from strong stems, not from the thin top wood. I have never liked this practice. I like to see the bushy shape of a rose tree in the summer. As far as I am concerned, it is sufficient to take away the old flowers down to the first leaf. The plant is quite capable of growing some new flowers without being barbed in high summer. Besides, all those lengths of stem contain food, and all those leaves thrown on to the rubbish heap are food-converting factories. Why throw them away? Just trim off the old heads, and watch the plant grow.

Disbudding This is not an essential; but when you are growing a large-flowered rose, it is pleasant to remove the side buds from a strong shoot. This does two things. By removing rival claimants for the food in the stem, it enables one flower to take the lot, and grow to unusual size and perfection; and as the side buds are not there to develop in their turn, eyes lower on the stem are prompted into growth a little sooner.

To be effective, disbudding must be done when the buds are very small, as soon as they can be handled easily. At this stage they are so tender, they snap off on being pulled downwards in an arc.

Cultivation During the spring and summer, it will be necessary to hoe your roses to defeat weeds. The alternative is to use a weed killer or suppressant, but those things are a little tricky; the hoe is cheaper and safer. Avoid damage to the plants, for it is through wounds that canker can enter your roses, slowly interrupting the passage of sap through the plant.

When the rose beds have been pruned, it is likely that the ground will be well trodden, and one will wish to tidy things up. There may even be some unpleasant weeds. Out come the tools, and it is at this stage that many a well meaning person has killed his roses with kindness. Rose roots often grow near the surface and certainly feeding roots do.

Therefore, never dig deeply among roses, because that is the way to destroy feeding roots and loosen main roots. Your spring digging ought to be shallow, probably no more than 2 or 3ins deep.

On some soils it is only necessary to chip the soil. If the ground will allow its use, a small sharp spade is a far better tool than a fork. If you catch a root with the tine of a fork, the whole length of it is loosened, whereas a spade cuts it clean, pruning it without disturbing it.

Feeding When the plants are established, they will certainly appreciate some extra food. Some sensible balance needs to be kept, so that the right foods are present, and timing is also important, lest there be waste one month and dearth the next.

Before recommending any programme, a sensible person would enquire as to the nature of the soil being thus reinforced. To add superfluity to abundance is just silly, and to withhold a missing essential sillier still.

Therefore I suggest a programme that ought to cover most eventualities, being based on the surmise that variety is the spice of life.

An obvious time to feed roses is just after pruning, when any substance may be conveniently applied, and subsequently worked into the ground with the spring cultivation. As the whole season stretches ahead, and the food will not be used immediately, a feed at this time needs to be a long and lasting one, and the three substances likely to be useful are manure, bone-meal and hoof-and-horn.

I suggest that only one of these be added in one season, so that over three seasons a varied diet is given. Manure needs to be well rotted, not fresh. It should be spread on top of the ground and then chipped into the soil with a spade. Bone-meal and hoof-and-horn are both perfectly safe fertilizers, with a long, low yield, feeding power. They should be spread on the ground about 4oz to the square yard, and then worked in with the spring cultivation.

In May the roses should be growing well, and coming into bud. At this stage they can well take a fertilizer. Every year some new speciality is being boosted, and if there is one you have confidence in, and if it is made by a reputable firm and recommended for roses, by all means try it. Use a little and often, never a lot once and no more. As one item in a three-year programme, Eclipse Fish Manure is excellent. The summer feeds could well be applied in May, June and July; the best results will come if they are applied on moist soil.

No more growth-promoting fertilizers should be used after July, but in August each year you could not go wrong in giving your plants 2oz of sulphate of potash to the square yard. This material will help the wood to ripen and stand the winter.

Many people grow beautiful roses without feeding them. When one knows the difference between roses ordinary and roses wonderful, it is hard to resist taking that little extra trouble to grow them wonderful.

11 Explaining the Rose List

A long list of varieties is not much fun to read; as literary enjoyment, it lacks the suspense of a well sustained plot, and most people would prefer Ian Fleming's style any day.

But it can be most valuable for reference, if it provides the information which will help. What is this information? Obviously, the colour, the height, and similar essential details we ought to know about roses before we plant them. Those who compile catalogues often omit to mention liability to disease, and resistance to bad weather. We can put all these useful things in this book.

The descriptions that follow will possess this basic outline:
1 Name of rose in bold type capitals
2 Colour in bold type
3 Average height in bold type
4 Vigour of the plant
5 Habit of the plant
6 Health
7 Amount and type of foliage
8 Colour of flower when young and old
9 Form and size of flower
10 Abundance of flowers
11 How flowers are carried
12 Weather resistance
13 Fragrance
14 The raiser
15 Date of introduction
16 Parentage
17 Other names for the rose

I need to explain these points. **The name** (1) is that registered and accepted by the Royal National Rose Society. **The colour** (2) is the predominant colour expressed shortly so that you can pick it out at a glance. **The average height** (3) is from my own observations, but I have already explained in this book that a rose can vary in height. **The vigour** (4) indicates the readiness of the plant to grow. Vigour does not mean height, but the ready production of shoots within the scope of the variety. I should say that a miniature rose such as 'Perla de Alcanada' is vigorous, whereas a tall plant that will not make new shoots is not vigorous.

The habit (5) means the shape of the plant. **The health** (6) is not so easy to tell, because a rose which gets mildew in Sussex may escape harm in the Black Country; for industrial smoke contains sulphur, and sulphur prevents mildew. You must therefore adapt this information to your own area. And of course I cannot promise that my observations will prove infallible in your garden. **The amount and type of foliage** (7) tells you whether the plant will be dense or sparse in leaf, and indicates the colour and shine. **The colour of flower when young and old** (8) will give a brief idea, avoiding high-flown fancy, of the colour at its best and worst. **The form and size of flower** (9) is quite straightforward; but please note that the expression single means a flower of five petals; semi-double roses open wide fairly soon, and double roses hold their centres to a later stage; the number of petals given is an average number. **Abundance of flowers** (10) gives an idea of the profusion when in full bloom, and the speed of repetition. **How flowers are carried** (11) should prove self-explanatory, and **Weather resistance** (12) ought to assist you to avoid those which seize up if you sneeze on them. That may be putting it rather high, but I well know the irritation people feel over roses which cannot take a shower of rain gracefully. **Fragrance** (13) is another variable factor, both as regards roses and noses. The other items (14–17) are put in just for interest.

How did I choose this list of roses? It is quite simple. They are all my favourite rose. People often ask me which is my favourite, and I usually reply I have a different favourite every day. If I had a garden large enough, I would grow all the roses in my list, and at any rate, if I could not fit them all in, I should choose from them.

Such a list will have additions every year, and at the end we have left space for you to fill in the roses you would like to add, so that your list may be complete.

ADAM MESSERICH   **Pink 6ft shrub**

Very vigorous; shrub, spreading out to two-thirds of height;
healthy; foliage ample, wide spaced, giving airy impression,
medium dull green; flowers deep pink, not fading much with
age; semi-double cupped shape; opening wide to 3ins diameter;
great profusion in summer flush, few thereafter; flowers in
terminal clusters of 3 to 5; weather resistance excellent; sweet
scent.
Raised by Peter Lambert, Trier, Germany. Introduced 1920.
Parentage: Frau Oberhofgärtner Singer × (Louise Odier
seedling × Louis Philippe).

ADELINE GENÉE   **Yellow 3ft bush**

Vigorous; bush, upright, with some extra strong shoots branching wide; slight mildew; foliage ample at base, little near
inflorescence, airy impression, light green, glossy; flowers clear
yellow, fading primrose; double, many petals, opening wide to
show well packed flower to 3½ins diameter; profuse in summer
and autumn flushes, scattered flower in between; flowers in
trusses of many blooms; weather resistance good; slight scent.
Raised by R. Harkness & Co. Ltd, Hitchin, Hertfordshire.
Introduced 1967. Parentage: Paddy McGredy × seedling.

A. F. HAHNE   **Pink/yellow 15ft climber**

Vigorous; climber, stiff stems, plenty of laterals; healthy;
foliage ample, medium green, glossy; flowers light pink, with
yellow and orange-yellow base, fading pale pink; semi-double,
high-centred bud, opening wide and loose to 3½ins diameter;
profuse early summer flush, rarely flowers later; flowers on
laterals in terminal clusters, usually 3; weather resistance good;
slight scent.
Raised by Kiese & Co., Viselbach-Erfurt, Germany. Introduced
1919.   Parentage: Unknown.

AFRICA STAR   Rosy mauve 1½ft bush

Moderately vigorous; bush, with spreading side shoots; black
spot likely; foliage abundant; middle green, dull; flowers rosy
mauve, very striking, not fading much; double, many petals,
holding a closed, sometimes quartered centre, opening to 3½ins
diameter; profuse in summer and autumn flushes, has long
flowering period; flowers in clusters, usually 3, sometimes in
large trusses spreading wide; weather resistance good; slight
scent.
Raised by Mrs Olga West, Que Que, Rhodesia. Introduced
1965. Parentage: Unknown.

ALAIN   Crimson 2½ft bush

Vigorous; bush, makes many shoots generally upright but
spreading out well; slight mildew; foliage abundant, close set,
middle green, glossy; flowers bright crimson, losing some
brilliance with age; semi-double; with about 25 small petals,
showing stamens; very profuse summer and autumn flushes,
scattered flowers through rest of season; flowers in trusses of
many blooms closely bunched; weather resistance good; scent
light but sweet.
Raised by Francis Meilland, Cap d'Antibes, France. Introduced
1946. Parentage: (Guinée × Wilhelm) × Orange Triumph.

ALAMEIN   Scarlet 2½ft bush

Vigorous; bush, fairly compact, spreads almost as wide as high;
slight mildew; foliage abundant, close set, middle green, matt;
flowers orange scarlet, vivid, fading crimson; semi-double, with
about 22 petals, loose centre, soon parting to open about 3½ins
in diameter; profuse in summer and autumn, with some flowers
in between; flowers in small clusters, sometimes singly, sometimes forms large trusses; weather resistance fair; scent faint
but sweet.
Raised by Sam McGredy, Portadown, Northern Ireland.
Introduced 1963. Parentage: Spartan × Queen Elizabeth.

ALBERIC BARBIER   Cream 25ft climber

Very vigorous; climber, makes several main shoots, which bear
long, rather pendulous branches; very healthy; foliage is

abundant, of small glossy leaves, bright medium green; stays on late; flowers pale cream, fading almost white with age; double, with about 30 petals, most of them small and folded in the centre; high-centred bud form, opening to 2½ins diameter with closed centre; profuse in early summer, scattered flower thereafter; flowers on side shoots, arising from wood made in former years, usually in terminal clusters of 3, sometimes more; weather resistance very good. Scent light but sweet.

Raised by Barbier & Co., Orleans, France. Introduced 1900. Parentage: *R. wichuraiana* × Shirley Hibberd.

ALBERTINE   Light pink 20ft climber

Extremely vigorous; climber, with many thorny shoots, growing fast; mildew likely; foliage very abundant, close set, semi-glossy, medium to deep green; flowers red in bud, light pink with touches of salmon as soon as they open, paler when old; double, high-centred when young, tightly held, opening with the centre closed, the petals showing points; opens to diameter of 3ins, and has up to 40 petals; flowers in tremendous profusion in early summer, very little thereafter; blooms are borne usually about 5 together on side shoots made from wood of former years; weather resistance good; scent strong and sweet.
Raised by Barbier & Co., Orleans, France. Introduced 1921. Parentage: *R. wichuraiana* × Mrs A. R. Waddell.

ALISON WHEATCROFT   Orange red 2ft bush

Moderately vigorous; bush, upright in growth, not spreading much; slight mildew and blackspot; foliage abundant, large, glossy dark green; flowers open orange, turn apricot, develop carmine edges; semi-double, petals loose, centre soon shows; up to 30 petals, and flower opens to 3ins diameter; profuse summer and autumn bloom, some in between; flowers either singly, or 3 to 5 together; weather resistance fair; scent light but sweet.
Discovered by Wheatcroft Bros, Ruddington, Nottingham. Introduced 1959. Parentage: Sport of Circus.

ALLEN CHANDLER   Crimson 8ft climber

Vigorous; climber, with stiff main shoots; healthy; foliage abundant, medium green, large, not dense, fairly glossy; flowers bright crimson, showing yellow stamens, hold colour well; semi-double, about 10 large petals, opening to show the centre, about 3½ins diameter; profuse in summer, with some flowers later; flowers on laterals made from old wood, also on young basal shoots, normally in clusters up to 5, sometimes more; weather resistance good; scent light but sweet.

Raised by Chandler. Introduced 1923 by Mr George Prince of Longworth, Berkshire. Parentage: Hugh Dickson × unknown.

ALLEN'S GOLDEN CLIMBER Apricot yellow 15ft climber

Extremely vigorous; climber, a dense plant, making thick, long shoots; very healthy; foliage very abundant, large, close set, medium green, fairly glossy; flowers are in between yellow and agricot in colour, fading paler with age; semi-double, with 7 or 9 large petals, opening to 4ins diameter; flowers early summer, spectacular but not profuse, no flowers thereafter; blooms on side shoots from old wood, usually in clusters of 3 or 5; weather resistance very good; scent sweet.

Raised by A. J. and C. Allen, Norwich. Introduced 1933. Parentage: Unknown. Was grown for some years under the name Hart's Single.

ALLGOLD Yellow 2½ft bush

Moderately vigorous; bush, spreading well, yet compact, free with its side shoots; healthy; foliage small, bright green, very glossy, fairly abundant; flowers are brilliant deep yellow, a little lighter when old; the buds are high centred, with 20–25 petals, opening to show the centre, and up to 3ins diameter; petals often scalloped; very profuse in bloom, giving three excellent flushes in the season; flowers in clusters of 3 or more on main shoots (occasionally in large trusses) or 1 to 3 on side shoots; weather resistance good; scent light but sweet.

Raised by E. B. le Grice, North Walsham, Norfolk. Introduced 1956. Parentage: Goldilocks × Ellinor le Grice.

ALLOTRIA Scarlet 3ft bush

Vigorous; bush, growing upright and spreading well; slight mildew; foliage abundant, deep green, fairly glossy; flowers orange scarlet, holding colour well; semi-double, about 12 crinkly petals, soon opening to 2ins diameter and showing centre; profuse summer and autumn bloom, with some in between; flowers in clusters of 3 to 5, sometimes singly; weather resistance good; scent faint.

Raised by Mathias Tantau, Uetersen, Germany. Introduced 1958. Parentage: Fanal × Tantau's Triumph seedling.

ALOHA   Pink 5ft climber

Moderately vigorous; not properly a climber, but a tall bush of upright growth which is grown as a short climber; healthy; foliage abundant, semi-glossy, dark green; flowers rose pink, holding their colour well; double, with 35 petals, high pointed centre while young, opening to loose-centred flower up to 4ins diameter; profuse summer flower, fair amount of bloom subsequently; borne in clusters, usually 3 together; weather resistance fairly good; scent sweet.

Raised by Eugene Boerner, Newark, New Jersey, USA. Introduced 1949. Parentage: Mercedes Gallart × New Dawn.

ALTISSIMO   Scarlet 12ft climber

Vigorous; climber, with stiff main shoots, apt to grow tall and flower high unless trained to the horizontal; healthy; foliage moderately abundant, semi-glossy, medium green, large; flowers brilliant deep scarlet, becoming crimson as they age; single, with about 7 large petals, opening to 4ins diameter, like a scarlet Mermaid; flowers scattered, summer flush moderately profuse, some fairly regularly thereafter; borne in clusters of usually 3 to 7 on side shoots from old wood; weather resistance good; scent light.

Raised by Delbard-Chabert, Paris, France. Introduced 1967. Parentage: Not known.

AMA   Crimson 2½ft bush

Vigorous; bush, compact, spreading well in proportion to height; healthy; foliage abundant, semi-glossy, dark green, dense; flower light crimson, bright, with darker edge to the petals, does not change much with age; semi-double, with 24 petals, opening to 3ins diameter; profuse summer and autumn flushes with some between; borne in trusses, well bunched, or

clusters of usually 5 together; weather resistance fair; faint
scent.
Raised by Wilhelm Kordes, Sparrieshoop, Germany. Introduced 1955. Parentage: Obergärtner Wiebicke × Independence.

AMERICAN PILLAR   Pink 20ft climber

Extremely vigorous; climber, producing many strong stems,
needs a large space; mildew likely; foliage very abundant,
large, close set, deep green, glossy; flowers carmine pink, with
white eye, fading to spotty pink; single, 5–7 petals, opening at
once to show the white eye, diameter about $1\frac{1}{4}$ins; extremely
profuse summer flowering, spectacular by its abundance,
scarcely any thereafter. Flowers in very large trusses of many
blooms, on side shoots from wood of former years; weather
resistance good; scent light.
Raised by Dr Walter van Fleet, Glenn Dale, Maryland, USA.
Introduced 1902. Parentage: (*R. wichuraiana* × *R. setigera*)
× red Hybrid Perpetual.

ANGELS MATEU   Pink/peach $2\frac{1}{2}$ft bush

Moderately vigorous; bush, upright and spreading well; slight
blackspot; foliage abundant, large and close set, glossy, deep
green; flowers rose pink with peach outer petals, holding the
colour well; double, with 35 petals, centre soon opens, diameter
4ins; very profuse in summer and autumn flower, some between;
flowers borne singly, or in clusters of 3; weather resistance
fairly good; scent sweet, fruity.
Raised by Pedro Dot, Barcelona, Spain. Introduced 1934.
Parentage: Magdalena de Nubiola × Duquesa de Penaranda.

ANNA WHEATCROFT   Salmon red $2\frac{1}{2}$ft bush

Vigorous; bush, upright, making many shoots and achieving
good spread; healthy; foliage abundant, dark green, semi-
glossy; flower colour is outside normal colour vocabulary,
attractive bright salmon red, darkening a little with age; semi-
double, with 12 petals, opening to 3ins diameter and showing
yellow stamens; profuse summer and autumn flushes, some in
between; flowers in clusters of about 5, often forms larger
heads; weather resistance good; scent faint.

Raised by Mathias Tantau, Uetersen, Germany. Introduced 1958. Parentage: Tantau's Triumph seedling × unknown.

ANNE LETTS   Pink 3ft bush

Vigorous; bush, upright, very thorny, makes few stems, with many side shoots; some mildew, slight blackspot; foliage fairly abundant, large, very glossy, middle green; flowers clear pale pink, cream deep in the centre, holding colour well; double flowers, large, up to 5ins diameter, of 30 big petals, the centre a well formed cone of petals, outer petals folding to points; flowers in moderate profusion summer and autumn, some in between; usually 3 to a shoot but often singly; weather resistance fair to poor; scent very sweet.

Raised by G. F. Letts & Sons, Hadleigh, Suffolk. Introduced 1953. Parentage: Peace × Charles Gregory.

ANN ELIZABETH   Pink 4ft bush

Very vigorous; bush, with long stems inclined to arch outwards; some mildew; slight blackspot; foliage abundant, rather small, glossy, bright deep green, gives bush airy appearance; flowers clear rose pink, taking red flecks with age; semi-double, of 20 petals, up to 3ins diameter, loosely formed; immensely profuse in summer and autumn, with some between; flowers in large heads, the individual stems of which are well spread apart, and bearing usually clusters of 7 to many; weather resistance fairly good; scent sweet.

Raised by Albert Norman, Normandy, Surrey. Introduced 1962. Parentage: Sheila Elizabeth × Queen Elizabeth.

ANNE POULSEN   Red 2½ft bush

Vigorous; bush, decidedly upright; healthy; foliage large, ample, semi-glossy; flower light crimson, darkening with age; semi-double, with about 9 large petals, opening wide to 3½ins diameter; profuse summer and autumn flushes, some between; flowers in large heads; weather resistance good.

Raised by Svend Poulsen, Copenhagen, Denmark. Introduced 1935. Parentage: Inger Olsson × seedling. Known in Europe as Anne-Mette Poulsen.

ANNE WATKINS
Cream/pink 2½ft bush

Moderately vigorous; bush, more upright than spreading; healthy; foliage dark green, semi-glossy, not over-abundant, giving airy appearance; flowers light creamy pink, with yellowish centre, some red flushes outside; holding colour well; double flowers, large, 5ins diameter, about 25 petals, well formed cone at centre; flowers freely summer and autumn, with some between; flowers singly, or 3 to a shoot; weather resistance very good; scent sweet.
Raised by Watkins Roses Ltd, Hampton-in-Arden, Warwickshire. Introduced 1963. Parentage: Ena Harkness × Grand'mère Jenny.

ARABIAN NIGHTS
Scarlet 3½ft bush

Very vigorous; bush, growing upright with handsome spread; some mildew; foliage glossy, dark green, coppery when young, abundant and dense; flowers bright scarlet, changing towards crimson when old; double, with high centre, 3½ins diameter, 28 petals; profuse summer and autumn bloom, some between; flowers usually in clusters of 3 or 5; weather resistance good; scent fairly perceptible.
Raised by Sam McGredy, Portadown, Northern Ireland. Introduced 1963. Parentage: Spartan × Beauté.

ARTHUR BELL
Yellow 3½ft bush

Vigorous; bush, fairly upright, apt to produce long shoots in summer; healthy; foliage ample, large, very glossy, light green; flowers bright yellow, fading cream white; double, with high centre when young, soon opening cup-shaped, 3½ins diameter; profuse flower summer and autumn, some between; flowers in clusters of 3 to 5, often in larger heads; weather resistance good; sweet scent.
Raised by Sam McGredy, Portadown, Northern Ireland. Introduced 1965. Parentage: Cläre Grammerstorf × Piccadilly.

AUSTRIAN COPPER
Yellow/red 5ft shrub

Moderately vigorous; shrub, with thin stems, spreads out as wide as high; blackspot likely; foliage ample, rather small, light green, matt, gives airy appearance; flowers orange scarlet within, yellow without, an intense colour, which does not have time to fade because the petals drop quickly; small single flowers with 5 petals; diameter about 1¼ins; profuse flower in early summer, when the bushes are fairly ablaze, no flowers thereafter; flowers on short stems arising from old wood, more frequently at the ends of the branches, but also further down; weather resistance is fair, but a heavy rain will quickly shatter the flowers; faint scent.

A variety of Austrian Yellow known in this country before 1590. Its botanical name is *Rosa foetida bicolor*.

AUSTRIAN YELLOW   Yellow 5ft shrub

Similar to Austrian Copper, except that the colour is rich yellow. This is a wild rose, native to Armenia, Kurdistan and North Persia, and introduced to this country before 1590.
Its botanical name is *Rosa foetida*.

BABY FAURAX   Lilac/mauve ¾ft bush

Not vigorous; bush, very short and stumpy, producing few shoots; healthy; foliage sparse, light green, matt; flowers deep and bright lilac mauve, becoming paler with age; semi-double flowers, rather less than 1 inch diameter, with 36 small petals soon opening to show the stamens; the summer flush is profuse, the autumn flowering rather more spasmodic; flowers in close heads of many flowers; weather resistance good; scent slight.
Raised by Leonard Lille, Lyon-Villeurbanne, France. Introduced 1924. Parentage: Unknown.

BABY MASQUERADE   Yellow/pink 1ft bush

Vigorous; bush, small, but very bushy with many shoots; healthy; foliage abundant, very small but close set, medium to deep green, semi-glossy; flowers light yellow with rose-pink tips to the petals, fading to predominantly light rose-red colour; semi-double flowers, with 28 petals, opening to show a confused centre; diameter about 1 inch; very profuse flower, in summer and autumn, usually quite a lot between; flowers in clusters of 3 to 12 usually; weather resistance good; scent faint.
Raised by Mathias Tantau, Uetersen, Germany. Introduced 1956. Parentage: Peon × Masquerade.

1 Guinevere

2 Golden Melody

3 King Arthur

4 Lady Hillingdon

5 Sterling Silver

6 Orange Sensation

7   Ena Harkness

8   *Rosa xanthina*

9   Allen Chandler

10 *Rosa scabrosa*

11 Charleston

12 Dandy Dick

13 Elizabeth of Glamis

14 Excalibur

15 Nevada

16 Glory of Ceylon

17 Rose Gaujard

18 Woburn Abbey

19 Lilli Marlene

20 Austrian Copper (*Rosa foetida bicolor*)

21 Joseph's Coat

22 Adeline Genee

23 Bourbon Queen

24 Frühlingsgold

BALLERINA   Pink 4ft shrub

Very vigorous; shrub, with many shoots, usually thin; upright
growth, spreading well; very healthy; foliage small, abundant,
medium to light green, semi-glossy, gives airy appearance;
flowers light pink, white at the centre, fading pale; single, about
1¼ins diameter, 5 to 7 petals, opening soon to show the white
eye; extremely profuse summer flower, with a very free repeat
in the autumn and some between; flowers in enormous heads
containing dozens of little flowers; weather resistance good;
light scent.
Raised by J. A. Bentall, Havering-atte-Bower, Essex. Introduced 1937. Parentage: Unknown, but as Mr Bentall took
over the Revd J. H. Pemberton's nursery, we may assume that
some of the Hybrid Musk breeding stock is behind Ballerina.

BALLET   Pink 3ft bush

Vigorous; bush, upright, with good spread; some blackspot;
foliage fairly abundant, leathery, middle green; flowers deep
rose pink, holding the colour well; double, tightly curled
petals, 45 of them, form a large flower with handsome centre,
sometimes split, up to 5ins diameter; free flowering summer
and autumn, some between; flowers singly, or several together,
but usually well apart; weather resistance excellent; sweet, but
light, scent.
Raised by Reimer Kordes, Sparrieshoop, Germany. Introduced
1958. Parentage: Florex × Karl Herbst.

BARBARA RICHARDS   Warm cream 2ft bush

Fairly vigorous; bush, basically upright but tries to grow
outward; some blackspot; foliage abundant, middle green,
close set, semi-glossy; flowers warm cream, with flushes of
pink, and in the autumn a touch of maize yellow; the colour
holds well; double, with 30 petals, forming a large bloom with
cone centre, superb form; free flowering in summer and autumn,
and some between; generally produced singly, but may be 3 or
more to a stem; the flowers tend to droop; weather resistance
good; scent strong and rich.
Raised by Alex. Dickson & Sons Ltd, Newtownards, Northern
Ireland. Introduced 1930. Parentage: Unknown.

BEAUTÉ   Peach yellow 2½ft bush

Vigorous; bush, upright with side shoots that spread well; healthy; foliage fairly abundant, glossy, deep green; flowers warm yellowish peach, opening from an orange bud, and holding the colour well; double, with 20 large petals forming rather a loose flower, which holds a good centre at the young stages; diameter up to 5ins; free flowering in summer and autumn, some between; generally produced singly, sometimes 3 or more to a stem; weather resistance good; sweet scent.

Raised by Charles Mallerin, Isère, France. Introduced 1953. Parentage: Mme Joseph Perraud × seedling.

BETTINA   Orange red 2½ft bush

Fairly vigorous; bush, upright, with many side shoots giving a good spread; subject to mildew and blackspot; foliage semi-glossy, dark green, showing coppery tints, abundant; flowers in sunshine warm peach, outer petals cream, showing orange veins; in cool weather deeper, more orange red, still veined; the colour holds well; double, with 30 petals, the centre well formed of petal tips close together; 4½ins diameter; free flowering in summer and autumn, some between; flowers on long straight stems, usually 3 to a shoot; weather resistance only fair; scent sweet but light.

Raised by Francis Meilland, Cap d'Antibes, France. Introduced 1953. Parentage: Peace × (Mme Joseph Perraud × Demain).

BETTY UPRICHARD   Pink 3ft bush

Very vigorous; bush, upright, usually of handsome, well filled character; healthy; foliage abundant, medium to light green, semi-glossy; flowers open light salmon pink with carmine reverse, from red buds; the colour holds well; semi-double, of 20 petals, close centre while young, up to 4ins diameter; profuse bloom summer and autumn, quite a few between; flowers singly or 3 to 5, sometimes more, per shoot; weather resistance excellent; light but sweet scent.

Raised by Alex. Dickson & Sons Ltd, Newtownards, Northern Ireland. Introduced 1922. Parentage: Unknown.

BLANC DOUBLE DE COUBERT White 3½ft bush

Very vigorous; shrub, with many thorny shoots, tends to spread rather wider than high; extremely healthy; foliage large, abundant, close set, light green, shiny, pale underneath, thick, very early to appear in spring; colour white; semi-double, opens flat, about 2½ins diameter, with 27 petals; free flowering in summer, produces quite a few scattered blooms thereafter; flowers in a cluster of up to 5 at or near the tip of the stem; weather resistance poor; scent strong and sweet.

Raised by Cochet-Cochet, Coubert, France. Introduced 1892. Parentage: *R. rugosa* × Sombreuil.

BLUE MOON Pinkish mauve 2½ft bush

Moderately vigorous; bush, firmly upright; healthy; foliage fairly abundant, semi-glossy, middle green; flowers light pinkish mauve, paling slightly with age; double, large, with 32 petals, good form, rather a loose cone at centre, diameter up to 4½ins; flowers freely summer and autumn, some in between; usually flowers singly or 3 to a stem, sometimes more; weather resistance fairly good; strong lemon scent.

Raised by Mathias Tantau, Uetersen, Germany. Introduced 1964. Parentage: Not known. The German name is Mainzer Fastnacht; also named Sissi, rather unkindly, I think.

BLUSH RAMBLER Light pink 15ft climber

Very vigorous; climber, with long thick shoots; some mildew; foliage very abundant, large, bright green, fairly glossy; flowers pale, blush pink, with deeper flushes, soon fading; semi-double, about 8 petals, cupped shape, showing stamens, 1½ins diameter; profuse summer flower, very little thereafter; flowers in large heads, close together, on side shoots made from wood of former years; weather resistance good; sweet scent.

Raised by B. R. Cant & Sons Ltd, Colchester, Essex. Introduced 1903. Parentage: Crimson Rambler × The Garland.

BOURBON QUEEN Pink 5ft shrub

Vigorous; shrub, upright and spreading out well; slight mildew; foliage abundant, deep green, dull; flowers bright deep pink, with deeper marks; fading slightly with age; semi-double, about 2½ins diameter, opening to show the centre; very profuse summer bloom, showy, with occasional flowers thereafter; flowers borne in clusters, several together; weather resistance good; sweet scent.

Raised by M. Mauget, Orleans, France. Introduced 1834. Parentage: Not known. Other names include: Queen of Bourbons, Reine des Îles Bourbon, Souvenir de la Princesse de Lamballe.

BREEZE HILL — Blush 10ft climber

Vigorous; climber, with long shoots, plenty of side growths, often slow to reach maximum development; healthy; foliage abundant, rather small, medium green, semi-glossy; flowers blush, deeper at centre, slight apricot shading, paler when old; double, with 50 petals, a full flower packed to the centre, diameter about 3ins; profuse in summer, occasional bloom thereafter; flowers in clusters of 3 or more on side shoots produced from wood of former years. Weather resistance fairly good; scent light but sweet.

Raised by Dr Walter van Fleet, Glenn Dale, Maryland, USA. Introduced 1926. Parentage: *R. wichuraiana* × Beauté de Lyon.

BRUNONII — Blush 25ft climber

Very vigorous; climber, with long, thick, soft shoots, growing very fast; healthy, but not perfectly hardy; foliage abundant, very large, light grey green with almost a pink flush, unusual; flowers blush, quickly fading white; single, with 5 petals, very small, 1 inch diameter, opening to show many stamens; profuse early summer bloom, rarely any thereafter; flowers in large heads containing dozens of flowers close together; weather resistance poor; strong sweet scent.

This is a wild rose found growing in the Himalayas. Introduced 1922. A near relation to the Musk Rose, it is sometimes listed as *R. moschata nepalensis*.

BUCCANEER — Yellow 4½ft bush

Very vigorous; bush, with strong straight shoots, a tendency to be upright, may even be trained taller on a pillar; healthy; foliage abundant, deep bright green, fairly glossy, large; flower bright yellow, does not fade much; semi-double, large flowers of 24 petals, good centre when young, soon opening to diameter up to 5ins, petals often irregularly indented; very profuse flushes summer and autumn, with quite a lot between; flowers are borne 3 to 5 on a shoot, sometimes more, and the main stems make many side shoots; weather resistance good; sweet scent.

Raised by H. C. Swim for Armstrong Nurseries, Ontario, California, USA. Introduced 1952. Parentage: Geheimrat Duisberg × (Max Krause × Capt. Thomas).

CALIFORNICA   Pinky lilac 6ft shrub

Vigorous; shrub, with many thin shoots, becoming dense, upright, forms a fairly thick bush, will spread by runners; very healthy; foliage abundant, rather small, dull deep green; flowers light bright pinky lilac, showing yellow stamens, not fading much; single, with 5 petals, small, attaining about 1 inch diameter, opening flat quickly; flowers spasmodically summer to autumn, not in profusion at one time, but shows colour over a long period; flowers borne sometimes in close heads containing many, or in clusters of 5 or more, both on new wood, and on side shoots from old wood; weather resistance good; light musky scent. This is a wild rose from western USA introduced from California in 1878.

CANARY BIRD   Yellow 5ft shrub

Vigorous; shrub, with many shoots, becoming dense and wide; very healthy; foliage abundant, leaves small, each consisting of about 11 dainty leaflets, close set, medium to light green, matt; flowers canary yellow, paling slightly with age; single, with 5 petals, many stamens immediately shown, diameter about 1½ins; profuse flush of bloom in early summer, 3 or 4 weeks before bedding roses, only an occasional flower thereafter; flowers are borne from side shoots made in previous years; short flower stalks up to an inch long arise from the eyes of those side shoots, thus covering the side shoot with flower and causing it to arch downwards by weight of bloom; weather resistance fairly good; pleasant, musky scent.

This is a wild rose from North China, Mongolia and Turkistan, introduced from China in 1907. The botanical name is *R. xanthina spontanea*.

CANTABRIGIENSIS   Cream yellow 7ft shrub

Very vigorous; shrub, growing tall strong stems and spreading
out to handsome proportions; very healthy; foliage abundant,
close set, leaves consisting of about 11 dainty, fern-like leaflets,
medium to light green, matt; flowers primrose to cream, fading
pale in strong sun; single, with 5 petals, immediately showing
the stamens, about 1½ins diameter; wonderfully profuse early
summer bloom, 3 or 4 weeks before the bedding roses, no
flowers thereafter; flowers borne along the side shoots made in
previous years on short stalks up to an inch long, thus covering
those side shoots with flower and causing them to arch downwards; weather resistance fairly good; light musky scent.
Raised at the Cambridge Botanic Gardens. Introduced 1931.
Parentage: *R. hugonis* × *R. sericea hookeri*. Also known as
R. pteragonis cantabrigiensis.

CAPRICE   Pink/cream 2½ft bush

Very vigorous; bush, of fairly upright growth, and many side
shoots; spreading out wide; slight blackspot; foliage very
abundant, semi-glossy, dark green with coppery tints; flowers
bright carmine pink to carmine red inside, pinky cream outside,
not fading much; semi-double, large, open-centred flower up to
5ins diameter; very profuse in summer and autumn, with
flowers between flushes; bears 3 to 5 large flowers to a shoot;
weather resistance good; scent light.
Raised by Francis Meilland, Cap d'Antibes, France. Introduced
1948. Parentage: Peace × Fantastique. Also known as Lady
Eve Price.

CAROLINE TESTOUT   Pink 2ft bush

Vigorous; bush, fairly upright, with good spreading habit;
healthy; foliage ample, dull light green; flowers bright rose
pink, not fading much; double, with loose but closed centre,
3½ins diameter, about 32 petals; profuse summer and autumn
bloom, with some between flushes; flowers borne singly or in
groups of 3 to 5; weather resistance good; sweet scent.
Raised by Joseph Pernet-Ducher, Venissieux-les-Lyon, Rhône,
France. Introduced 1890. Parentage: Mme de Tartas × Lady
Mary Fitzwilliam. Official name is Mme Caroline Testout.

CASINO   Yellow 10ft climber

Vigorous; climber, with firm stems not too stiff for easy training; slight mildew; foliage sufficient, glossy, dark green, handsome; flowers yellow with a few red markings on outside
petals, do not fade much; double, with 50 petals closely packed,
loose but shapely centre, diameter 3½ins; flowers summer and
autumn, with quite a few in-between flushes; flowers borne
on side shoots from wood of former years, also terminally on
new main shoots, in clusters usually 3 to 5, sometimes more;
weather resistance good; sweet, rather soapy scent.
Raised by Sam McGredy, Portadown, Northern Ireland.
Introduced 1963. Parentage: Coral Dawn × Buccaneer.
Known in France as Gerbe d'Or.

CÉCILE BRUNNER   Pink 2ft bush

Moderately vigorous; bush, with thin shoots, rarely dense, but
spreading well; healthy; foliage medium green, fairly abundant,
leaves pointed, semi-glossy; flowers light rose pink with the
centre light salmon pink, pale when fully open; double, with
45 small petals; those at the centre narrow and folded; opens
with exquisite centre, like miniature Hybrid Tea, flower is only
1 inch or so in diameter; flowers summer to autumn, not so much
profuse as continuous; bears groups of 3 to 7 flowers on the
stronger shoots, often makes small shoots bearing one bloom;
weather resistance very good; light but sweet scent.
Raised by Veuve Ducher, Lyon, Rhône, France. Introduced
1881. Parentage: thought to be a Polyantha × Mme de Tartas.
Has been listed as Mignon, Mme Cécile Brunner, Mlle Cécile
Brunner, Sweetheart Rose.
Note: A more vigorous strain is often sold as this variety,
growing about 4ft tall, with huge, airy heads of flower. The
two strains ought really to have separate identification, but
this has never been done as far as I know, except by calling
the taller one Bloomfield Abundance; but if the parentage
record of Bloomfield Abundance is correct, then that must be a
different rose altogether.

CÉCILE BRUNNER CLIMBING   Pink 20ft climber

Similar to Cécile Brunner, except in these respects: very
vigorous; climber, with long, strong shoots; flowers profusely

in summer, not much thereafter; flowers on side shoots growing from wood made in former years.
Discovered by F. P. Hosp, Riverside, California, USA. Introduced 1894. Parentage: Sport of Cécile Brunner.

CELEBRATION
Salmon 2½ft bush

Vigorous; bush, upright with good spreading habit, not stiff; healthy; foliage fairly abundant, semi-glossy, middle green; flowers salmon red inside, lighter outside, fading paler; semi-double, with 26 petals, holding good form when young, opening to 3½ins diameter to show loose centre; extremely prolific summer and autumn flushes, with some flower in between; flowers in close heads, usually 5 or more to a stem; weather resistance good; light but sweet scent.
Raised by Patrick Dickson, Newtownards, Northern Ireland. Introduced 1961. Parentage: Dickson's Flame × Circus.

CHAMPS-ELYSÉES
Crimson 2½ft bush

Vigorous; bush, upright and compact, spreading neatly; healthy; foliage abundant, middle green, semi-glossy; colour bright crimson scarlet, loses some brightness with age; double, with 35 petals, good cone at centre when young, but soon opens to 4½ins diameter; free flowering in summer and autumn, with occasional flowers between flushes; flowers are borne usually 3 to a stem, sometimes 1; weather resistance good; sweet scent.
Raised by Francis Meilland, Cap d'Antibes, France. Introduced 1957. Parentage: Monique × Happiness.

CHANELLE
Blush 2½ft bush

Vigorous; bush, with free spreading habit; healthy; foliage abundant, glossy light bronze green; flowers start as orange buds, opening cream with yellow in the centre, and blush pink outer petals; when old, the flowers are light blush pink; semi-double, 20 petals, soon showing centre, 3½ins diameter; flowers abundantly summer and autumn, with quite a few in between flushes; flowers normally in clusters of 3 or 5; weather resistance good; scent pleasant.
Raised by Sam McGredy, Portadown, Northern Ireland. Introduced 1959. Parentage: Ma Perkins × (Fashion × Mrs William Sprott).

CHAPLIN'S PINK CLIMBER   Bright pink 15ft climber

Very vigorous; climber, with many strong shoots, fast growing, needs room; healthy; foliage very abundant, rounded leaves, very glossy, dark green; flowers bright deep pink, a strong colour; semi-double, about 13 petals, soon show stamens, diameter 2ins; very abundant flower in summer, very little thereafter; flowers on side shoots from wood made in former years, usually in clusters of 5 or 7, sometimes in large heads; weather resistance fairly good; faint scent.
Raised by Chaplin Bros, Ltd, Waltham Cross, Hertfordshire. Introduced 1928. Parentage: Paul's Scarlet Climber × American Pillar.

CHAPLIN'S PINK COMPANION   Pink 10ft climber

Vigorous; climber, with firm shoots quite easy to train; slight mildew; foliage abundant, semi-glossy, medium to dull green; flowers light pink, slightly yellow at base, paler when old; semi-double, with about 18 petals, soon showing centre, up to 2ins diameter; wonderful abundant flower in early summer, very little thereafter; flowers from side shoots arising from wood of former years in clusters of 5 or more, and in large heads; weather resistance quite good; pleasant light scent.
Raised by H. J. Chaplin, Cheshunt, Hertfordshire. Introduced 1961. Parentage: Chaplin's Pink Climber × Opera.

CHARLESTON   Red/yellow 2ft bush

Vigorous; bush, of low, compact habit; very liable to blackspot; abundant foliage, bright bronze green, glossy; flowers yellow and red, the colours brilliant, invading one another, yellow from centre of flower and on outside of petals, fading pale, the red colour fading dull crimson; semi-double, opening to 2½ins diameter, with 20 petals, soon showing centre, opening from neat bud to rather untidy flower; abundant summer and autumn bloom, some between flushes; flowers normally in large heads; weather resistance quite good; slight scent.
Raised by Alain Meilland, Cap d'Antibes, France. Introduced 1963. Parentage: Masquerade × Banzai.

CHARLOTTE ELIZABETH   Deep pink 3½ft bush

Vigorous; bush, decidedly upright; healthy; foliage abundant, middle green, slightly glossy; flowers deep reddish pink, not fading much; semi-double with 22 petals, holding excellent centres until late stage, 3½ins diameter; flowers profusely summer and autumn, quite a few between flushes; blooms in even heads of 5 or many; weather resistance good; scent light but sweet.

Raised by Albert Norman, Normandy, Surrey. Introduced 1965. Parentage: Sheila Elizabeth × Queen Elizabeth.

CHARM OF PARIS   Pink 2½ft bush

Vigorous; bush, upright and spreading quite wide; healthy; foliage very abundant, fairly glossy, deep green; flowers clear salmon pink, paler when old; double, with about 40 petals, rather rounded centre, 3ins diameter; flowers freely summer and autumn, some between flushes; carries clusters of flowers on rather weak flower stalks, usually 5 together; weather resistance mediocre; scent strong and rich.

Raised by Mathias Tantau, Uetersen, Germany. Introduced 1966. Parentage: Unknown.

CHINATOWN   Yellow 5ft shrub

Very vigorous; bush, spreading wide, with strong shoots, and the compass of the plant well filled in; healthy; foliage very abundant, glossy, large, bright green; flowers bright yellow, outer petals paler, does not fade much; double flowers, of 40 petals, well formed, with cone at centre, petals sometimes scalloped, diameter 3½ins; free flowering in summer, with generous subsequent bloom and a fair flush in autumn; flowers in clusters usually of 3 to 5 to a shoot; weather resistance fair; rich, lemon scent.

Raised by Niels Poulsen, Kvistgaard, Denmark. Introduced 1963. Parentage: Columbine × Cläre Grammerstorf.

CIRCUS   Yellow/pink 2ft bush

Fairly vigorous; bush, more upright than spreading; slight blackspot; foliage fairly abundant, glossy, medium green with bluish tinge; flower opens orange, turns yellow with carmine flushes and pink edges; pleasing even when old; double, with about 32 petals tightly packed, and forming a pretty centre at the young stages; diameter 3ins; flowers profusely in summer and autumn, with some between flushes; weather resistance fairly good; scent light but sweet.

Raised by H. C. Swim for Armstrong Nurseries, Ontario, California, USA. Introduced 1956. Parentage: Fandango × Pinocchio. Note: A coarser growing light coloured strain of Circus is also in existence.

COLUMBINE Cream/pink 2½ft bush

Vigorous; bush, with spreading growth, good shaped plant; healthy; foliage abundant, glossy bright green; flower pale cream, with pink marks particularly at the petal edges; the colour is more yellow at times, and does not fade much; double flowers, with 40 petals, holding a well formed centre at the young stages, opening to 3½ins diameter; very free flowering summer and autumn, with some bloom between flushes; flowers in clusters of 3 to 5 together, sometimes more; weather resistance fair; sweet, light scent.

Raised by Svend Poulsen, Copenhagen, Denmark. Introduced 1956. Parentage: Danish Gold × Frensham.

COPPER DELIGHT Light orange 2½ft bush

Fairly vigorous; bush, with rather open growth, spreading well; slight blackspot; foliage rather sparse, glossy, bright green, gives open appearance to plant; flowers are clear orange soon fading to light orange, and paler when old; semi-double, with about 12 petals, showing the centre soon, remaining slightly cup shaped most of the time, diameter about 3ins; very abundant summer and autumn flushes, some in between; flowers in clusters of 5 usually, but also in heads containing many blooms; weather resistance very good; pleasant musky scent.

Raised by E. B. le Grice, North Walsham, Norfolk. Introduced 1956. Parentage: Goldilocks × Ellinor le Grice.

CORNELIA Coppery pink 5ft shrub

Very vigorous; shrub, with arching stems, spreading wider than high; very healthy; foliage abundant, glossy, dark green, close set; flowers light pink, in which the coppery shades of the young flowers fade to apricot with age; double, with 42 small petals, keeping the centre closed while young, diameter about $1\frac{3}{4}$ins; very free flowering, with good summer and autumn flushes, and rarely without a bloom in between; flowers in clusters of 3 or more, also in sprays of many; weather resistance good; sweet scent.

Raised by Revd J. H. Pemberton, Havering-atte-Bower, Essex. Introduced 1925. Parentage: Unknown.

CRIMSON SHOWER   Crimson 8ft climber

Vigorous; climber, with very pendulous, thin stems; healthy; foliage small, very abundant, close set, very glossy, bright light green; flowers bright crimson, some white markings, become dull with age; double, with closed centre, 30 small petals making rosette flower up to 2ins diameter; very prolific; late summer flowering only; flowers in clusters of 7 to 15 close together, and in larger heads; weather resistance fair; faint scent.

Raised by Albert Norman, Normandy, Surrey. Introduced 1951. Parentage: Excelsa seedling.

CYNTHIA BROOKE   Peach yellow 2ft bush

Fairly vigorous; bush, upright and spreading outwards; black-spot likely; foliage abundant, glossy, light green; flower strong yellow, tinged with peach, especially on outside of petals, does not fade much; double, with rather rounded centre, 50 petals, opens to $4\frac{1}{2}$ins diameter; abundant summer and autumn flushes, some flowers in between; flowers either 1 or 3 to a stem usually; weather resistance fair; scent fruity.

Raised by S. McGredy & Son Ltd, Portadown, Northern Ireland. Introduced 1943. Parentage: Le Progrès × (Mme Melanie Soupert × Le Progrès).

DAINTY BESS   Pink $2\frac{1}{2}$ft bush

Fairly vigorous; bush, upright, not spreading much; healthy; foliage rather sparse, middle green, semi-glossy; flowers light rose pink, showing dark stamens; single, with 5 large petals, about $3\frac{1}{2}$ins diameter; free flowering in summer and autumn, with a few between flushes; flowers in groups of 3 to 7 on a stem, and in larger heads; weather resistance fair; fresh scent.

Raised by W. E. B. Archer, Sellindge, Kent. Introduced 1925.
Parentage: Ophelia × K. of K.

DAINTY MAID   Pink 3ft bush

Vigorous; bush, decidedly upright, but with sufficient shoots
to make a wide, substantial plant; healthy; foliage abundant,
pleasing medium green, semi-glossy; flowers open clear rose
pink from a red bud, and soon show attractive stamens; paler
with age; single, with about 7 petals, opening to 2½ins diameter; extremely free flowering in summer and autumn, with
some between flushes; flowers in large heads of many flowers
on the main shoots, usually in clusters of 3 to 5 on side shoots;
weather resistance quite good; scent light.
Raised by E. B. le Grice, North Walsham, Norfolk. Introduced
1938. Parentage: D. T. Poulsen × unknown.

DANDY DICK   Pink 3ft bush

Vigorous; bush, upright, spreading well, as wide as high; very
healthy; foliage very abundant, light green, matt; flowers clear
rose pink, fade hardly at all; double, with 25 petals, very straight
and attractive centre held to a late stage, diameter 3½ins;
abundant flower in summer and autumn, many between
flushes; flowers in clusters of 3 to 5, or in larger heads occasionally; weather resistance very good; light, spicy scent.
Raised by R. Harkness & Co. Ltd, Hitchin, Hertfordshire.
Introduced 1967. Parentage: Pink Parfait × Red Dandy.

DANSE DES SYLPHES   Scarlet 10ft climber

Vigorous; climber, with fairly upright stems; healthy; foliage
fairly abundant, glossy, middle green; flowers orange scarlet,
the outer petals in particular fading pale crimson with age;
double, with 36 petals, rather rounded form, loose centre,
diameter 3ins; profuse summer flush, with good scattering
of later bloom; flowers usually 5 to a cluster on side shoots from
the wood of former years; weather resistance fair; scent faint.
Raised by Charles Mallerin, Isère, France. Introduced 1957.
Parentage: Danse du Feu × (Peace × Independence).

DANSE DU FEU   Scarlet 10ft climber

Vigorous; climber, with strong stems, but easy to train;
healthy; foliage fairly abundant, glossy, middle to deep green;
flowers scarlet to crimson, fading crimson purple with age;
semi-double, with about 23 petals, loose centre, soon opening
from good bud form to diameter 3ins; profuse summer flush,
with good amount of later flower to autumn; flowers in clusters
of about 7 both on side shoots and young main shoots; weather
resistance fair; scent faint.
Raised by Charles Mallerin, Isère, France. Introduced 1954.
Parentage: Paul's Scarlet Climber × *R. multiflora* seedling.
Name in USA is Spectacular.

DEAREST   Pink 2½ft bush

Vigorous; bush, upright habit with excellent spread; may get
blackspot and rust; foliage fairly abundant, glossy, dark green;
flower warm salmon pink, fades a little lighter with age; double,
with 28 petals, closely formed flower of rosette type, opening
flat to diameter of 3ins; flowers in clusters of 3 or more, several
such clusters to a stem; weather resistance rather poor; scent
strong and pleasant.
Raised by Alex. Dickson & Sons Ltd, Newtownards, Northern
Ireland. Introduced 1960. Parentage: Seedling × Spartan.

DECAPO   Salmon 1½ft bush

Vigorous; bush, short in growth, rather upright; healthy;
foliage rather sparse, middle green, matt; flowers clear bright
salmon pink, fading a little with age; semi-double, well formed
young flower, 27 petals, loose centre, opening to 3ins diameter;
very free flowering summer and autumn, a few between flushes;
weather resistance good; scent light but sweet.
Raised by G. de Ruiter, Hazerswoude, Holland. Introduced
1963. Parentage: Unknown.

DESPERADO   Yellow/pink 3ft bush

Vigorous; bush, upright, spreading wide into a well rounded
plant; healthy; foliage ample, rather narrow, deep green, semi-
glossy; flower yellow, shaded pink on outer petals, fades pale;
semi-double, 12 petals, soon shows centre, 2ins diameter;

very abundant in flower, summer and autumn flushes both profuse, with quite a lot in between; flowers in clusters of several to a stem, sometimes in large heads, also singly on short shoots; weather resistance good; scent faint.
Raised by R. Harkness & Co. Ltd, Hitchin, Hertfordshire. Introduced 1968. Parentage: Pink Parfait × Masquerade.

DIAMOND JUBILEE   Deep cream 2½ft bush

Vigorous; bush, upright, spreading well, dense plant; mildew likely; foliage abundant, semi-glossy, middle green; flowers warm cream, sometimes light maize, fading paler; double, with 35 petals, large well formed flower with cone at centre, opening to 5ins diameter; flowers freely summer and autumn, some between flushes; bears flowers singly or 3 per stem; weather resistance only fair; rich, sweet scent.
Raised by Eugene Boerner, Newark, New Jersey, USA. Introduced 1947. Parentage: Maréchal Niel × Feu Pernet-Ducher.

DIORAMA   Yellow 2½ft bush

Vigorous; bush, upright and spreading well; healthy; foliage abundant, semi-glossy, handsome, dark green; flower deep yellow with pink tinges, does not fade much; double, with 25 petals, well formed and large, high cone at centre while young; opens to 4½ins diameter; free summer and autumn flushes, with some regularly in between; often flowers singly, or 3 to a stem; weather resistance good; sweet scent.
Raised by G. de Ruiter, Hazerswoude, Holland. Introduced 1965. Parentage: Peace × Beauté.

DIREKTOR BENSCHOP   White 15ft climber

Vigorous; climber, with rather pendulous stems; healthy; foliage abundant, medium green, glossy; flowers open cream, fade white; semi-double, 15 petals, soon show centre, open to 2ins diameter; abundant summer flower, little thereafter; flowers in clusters of 5 to many; weather resistance good; slight sweet scent.
Raised by Mathias Tantau, Uetersen, Germany. Introduced 1945. Parentage: Professor Gnau × Dorothy Perkins. Named City of York in USA.

DOROTHY PEACH   Yellow 2½ft bush

Vigorous; bush, upright of restrained spread; healthy; foliage
abundant, glossy, middle green; flowers clear yellow, pink
tinges on the outer petals, do not fade much; double, well
formed, 26 petals, closed shapely centre, opening to 4½ins
diameter; free flowering in summer and autumn, sparse flower
between flushes; flowers 1 to 3 per stem; weather resistance
fair; sweet scent.
Raised by Herbert Robinson, MBE, Burbage, Leicestershire.
Introduced 1957. Parentage: Lydia × Peace.

DOROTHY WHEATCROFT   Scarlet 5ft shrub

Vigorous; shrub, upright, not much lateral spread, rather open
plant; healthy; foliage abundant, glossy, middle green; flowers
bright orange scarlet, fading with pink tinge; semi-double,
with 15 petals, loose centre, scalloped edges, opening to 3ins
diameter; prolific summer and autumn bloom, some between
flushes; flowers in large heads, several flowers close together
filling the inflorescence with spectacular colour; weather
resistance good; faint sweet scent.
Raised by Mathias Tantau, Uetersen, Germany. Introduced
1961. Parentage: Unknown.

DR W. VAN FLEET   Blush 20ft climber

Very vigorous; climber, with many shoots, and some of the
laterals very long; healthy; foliage ample, small, very glossy,
bright middle green; flowers pale blush pink, not fading much;
semi-double, with small cone centre in young flowers, 24 petals,
opening to 3ins diameter; extremely profuse summer flower,
not much thereafter; flowers on side shoots from old wood in
clusters of 5 to 11 usually; weather resistance good; sweet rich
scent.
Raised by Dr W. van Fleet, Glenn Dale, Maryland, USA.
Introduced 1910. Parentage: (*R. wichuraiana* × Safrano) ×
Souv. de Président Carnot. Except in habit of growth and
period of bloom, this rose is the same as New Dawn.

DUPONTII   White 5ft shrub

Very vigorous; shrub, spreading as wide as high in excellent
well filled form; healthy; foliage abundant, greyish green, matt;

flowers open white from pink buds, do not fade; single, with
5 petals, opening flat to 2½ins diameter, showing yellow stamens;
extremely profuse flower smothers the bush in summer,
scarcely any thereafter; flowers in clusters of 4 to 7 on shoots
produced from wood of former years; weather resistance good;
fresh light scent.

Origin unknown, but thought to have been from *R. gallica* ×
R. moschata, or more probably from hybrids of one or both. In
cultivation prior to 1817.

ÉBLOUISSANT   Red 1½ft bush

Vigorous; bush, with short shoots and compact growth; very
healthy; foliage abundant, small, bronze to middle green,
glossy; flowers red, towards crimson, bright, losing brightness
with age; semi-double with about 20 petals, showing centre
soon, opening to 1½ins diameter; free flowering summer flush,
fairly good autumn flush, good continuity of spasmodic flower
in between; flowers in clusters of 3 to 5 usually; weather
resistance good; slight scent.

Raised by E. Turbat & Co., Orleans, France. Introduced 1918.
Parentage: Unknown × Cramoisie Supérieur.

EDEN ROSE   Pink 3½ft bush

Vigorous; bush, upright, apt to produce occasional shoot taller
than the rest; mildew likely; foliage abundant, glossy, dark
green; flowers deep pink from carmine bud, do not fade
much; double, very large flower of 50 petals, with closed
centre, tightly formed, sometimes split by petal folds, opening
to 5ins diameter; free flowering in summer and autumn, some
between flushes; flowers produced singly, often with side buds
following; weather resistance good; sweet scent.

Raised by Francis Meilland, Cap d'Antibes, France. Introduced
1950. Parentage: Peace × Signora.

ELEGANCE   Cream yellow 20ft climber

Very vigorous indeed; climber, with long, thick, thorny shoots,
not easy to train in small space; healthy; foliage abundant,
apart from plant base, bright green, glossy; flower cream with
yellow inwardly, fading white at edges; double flowers, 45
petals, beautiful straight centres, holding form late, opening

7—GR

to 4ins diameter; profuse summer flower, when the plant is
a magnificent sight, rarely any thereafter; flowers 3 to 7 on side
shoots coming from wood of former years; weather resistance
good; slight scent.
Raised by Dr & Mrs Walter Brownell, Little Compton, Rhode
Island, USA. Introduced 1937. Parentage: Glenn Dale ×
(Mary Wallace × Miss Lolita Armour).

ELFE   **Blush 3ft bush**

Very vigorous; bush, upright, but not stiff, and spreads out
well; very healthy; foliage very abundant, glossy, bright green;
flowers very pale blush, almost white, developing pink flecks
with age; semi-double, with 10 petals, loose formation, opening
flat to $3\frac{1}{2}$ins diameter, scalloped petal edges; extremely profuse,
both in summer and autumn, with some flowers between
flushes; flowers in clusters of 3 to 7 usually, sometimes many
on a strong main shoot; weather resistance fair; scent sweet.
Raised by Mathias Tantau, Uetersen, Germany. Introduced
1951. Parentage: Swantje × Hamburg.

ELIZABETH OF GLAMIS   **Pink/orange $2\frac{1}{2}$ft bush**

Moderately vigorous; bush, decidedly upright; some liability
to diseases; foliage moderately abundant, semi-glossy, middle
green; flowers salmon pink, shaded apricot and orange, very
beautiful, do not fade much; double, with 28 petals, well
formed with cone at centre, eventually opening to 4ins diameter; prolific in summer and autumn, good few in between;
flowers in heads of 5 or more, sometimes of 3 on side shoots;
weather resistance fairly good; scent sweet.
Raised by Sam McGredy, Portadown, Northern Ireland.
Introduced 1964. Parentage: Spartan × Highlight.

ENA HARKNESS   **Crimson $2\frac{1}{2}$ft bush**

Moderately vigorous; bush, fairly upright; healthy; foliage
moderately abundant, semi-glossy, medium green; flowers
bright deep crimson, do not fade much; double, with 26 petals;
large and excellently formed with regular centre from which
petal tips bend back, opening to $4\frac{1}{2}$ins diameter; very free
flowering summer and autumn, also some between flushes;

flowers singly or 3 to 7 per stem, flowers tend to droop; weather resistance good; strong lemon scent.
Raised by Albert Norman, Normandy, Surrey. Introduced 1946. Parentage: Crimson Glory × Southport.

ENA HARKNESS CLIMBING   Crimson 10ft climber

Similar to Ena Harkness except in these respects: climber, easy to train; flowers freely in summer, only a few thereafter; flowers on side shoots from wood made in former years.
Discovered by Worth Park Nurseries, Horley, Surrey, and R. Murrell, Hemel Hempstead, Hertfordshire, in the same year. Introduced 1954. Parentage: Sport of Ena Harkness.

ERNEST H. MORSE   Crimson 3ft bush

Vigorous; bush, rather open in habit, of upright growth and spreading; healthy; foliage abundant, semi-glossy, deep green; flowers scarlet turning to crimson; double, large flowers, of 35 petals, well formed though the centre is loose; opening to 4½ins diameter; free flowering in summer and autumn, with some between flushes; flowers usually 1 or 3 to a stem, sometimes more on strong shoots; weather resistance good; sweet scent.
Raised by Wilhelm Kordes, Sparrieshoop, Germany. Introduced 1964. Parentage: Unknown.

ESCAPADE   Magenta/rose 2½ft bush

Vigorous; bush, rather open in habit, upright, spreading moderately; healthy; foliage abundant, light green, glossy; flowers magenta rose with white centre, showing yellow stamens; semi-double, with 12 petals, showing white centre, opening not quite flat to 2½ins diameter; very free flowering summer and autumn, some between flushes; flowers in large heads, or 3 to 5 on side shoots, the flowers held up to view very sweetly; weather resistance fairly good; musky scent.
Raised by R. Harkness & Co. Ltd, Hitchin, Hertfordshire. Introduced 1967. Parentage: Pink Parfait × Baby Faurax.

ÉTOILE DE HOLLANDE CLIMBING Crimson 15ft climber

Vigorous, though may be slow to start; climber, fairly stiff stems, quite easy to train; healthy; foliage ample, semi-glossy, deep green; flowers crimson, fading slightly purple with age; semi-double, with 24 petals, parting rather soon at centre, opening large to 4ins diameter; very profuse summer bloom, little thereafter; flowers usually 3 to a stem, on side shoots produced from wood of former years; weather resistance good; scent rich and sweet.

Discovered by M. Leenders & Co., Tegelen, Holland. Introduced 1931. Parentage: Sport of Étoile de Hollande.

EUROPEANA   Crimson 2ft bush

Vigorous; bush, rather lax and spreading out readily; mildew very likely; foliage abundant, dark green, coppery when young, very glossy; flowers bright deep crimson, striking; double, with 36 petals forming a circular rosette, diameter 3ins; profuse summer and autumn bloom, some between flushes; flowers in heads of 7 to 13 usually, sometimes many; weather resistance fair, heavy rain makes the flowers droop; slight scent.

Raised by G. de Ruiter, Hazerswoude, Holland. Introduced 1963. Parentage: Ruth Leuwerik × Rosemary Rose.

EVENSONG   Salmon pink 3ft bush

Vigorous; bush, upright, spreading a little; healthy; foliage abundant, large leaves, middle green, matt; flowers open clear deep salmon pink from scarlet-pink buds; they do not fade much; double, with 26 petals, straight centre while young, opening to 5ins diameter; profuse summer and autumn bloom, some between flushes; flowers usually 3 to a stem, the stems straight, firm and slim; weather resistance fairly good; strong sweet scent.

Raised by David Arnot, Dundee, Scotland. Introduced 1963. Parentage: Ena Harkness × Sutter's Gold.

EXCALIBUR   Scarlet 2ft bush

Vigorous; bush, spreads as wide as high; fairly healthy; foliage moderately abundant, deep green, very shiny; flowers startling scarlet, fade crimson; semi-double, 14 petals, open soon to show yellow stamens, 2½ins diameter; very profuse flower summer and autumn, some between; flowers in clusters of 3 to 7, sometimes larger heads; weather resistance fairly good; slight scent.

Raised by R. Harkness & Co. Ltd, Hitchin, Hertfordshire. Introduced 1967. Parentage: Vera Dalton × Woburn Abbey.

FÉLICITÉ ET PERPÉTUE   White 12ft climber

Vigorous; climber, with slim long branches, easy to train; very healthy; foliage abundant, greyish green, matt; flowers white with slight blush, do not fade; very double, small flowers with about 50 tiny petals in beautiful rosette form, 1½ins diameter; very profuse bloom early summer, little thereafter; flowers in clusters of 3 to many, on side shoots produced from wood of former years; weather resistance good; sweet scent.
Raised by A. A. Jacques, Chateau de Neuilly, France. Introduced 1827. Parentage: Sport of *R. sempervirens*.

FIRST CHOICE   Orange red 3½ft bush

Very vigorous; bush, upright with purposeful spread outwards; healthy; foliage abundant, deep green, semi-glossy; flowers orange carmine inside, yellowish cream outside, vivid; lose brightness with age; single, with 5 or 6 petals, opening wide to 4ins diameter; free flowering summer and autumn, some between flushes; flowers singly or 3 to a stem, occasionally more; weather resistance good; faint scent.
Raised by Henry Morse & Sons, Norwich. Introduced 1958. Parentage: Masquerade × Sultane.

FRAGRANT CLOUD   Scarlet 2½ft bush

Vigorous; bush, upright and spreading well; healthy; foliage abundant, large, dense, glossy, dark green with copper tint; flowers bright carmine scarlet, fading rather purple red; double, with 30 petals, very well formed with closed centre, opening to a large flower of 4½ins diameter; very profuse bloom summer and autumn, with a good supply between flushes; flowers singly, or more usually 3 to 5 on a stem, sometimes produces a large head of flowers; weather resistance fairly good; very strong rich scent.
Raised by Mathias Tantau, Uetersen, Germany. Introduced 1963. Parentage: Seedling × Prima Ballerina. Known in Germany as Duftwolke; in France as Nuage Parfumé.

FRANÇOIS JURANVILLE   Pink 20ft climber

Vigorous; climber, with long pendulous shoots; healthy; foliage
abundant, usually covers base of plant well, small, glossy, dark
green; flowers rose pink with touch of yellow at base, a little
paler with age; semi-double with about 20 small petals, opening
to 1½ins diameter; very profuse summer bloom, scarcely any
thereafter; flowers in clusters of 3 to 7 normally, on thin side
shoots arising from old wood; flowers are well spaced on plant
to show bright foliage backing them; weather resistance good;
sweet scent.

Raised by Barbier & Co., Orléans, France. Introduced 1906.
Parentage: *R. wichuraiana* × Mme Laurette Messimy.

FRAU KARL DRUSCHKI   White 4ft bush

Vigorous; bush, upright, occasionally sends out very long
shoots, spreads moderately outwards; some mildew; foliage
ample, light green, matt; flowers white, often with pink tinge,
sometimes red flush on outer petals, little fading; double, with
35 large petals forming excellent cone centre, large, opening
to 5ins diameter; profuse summer bloom, spasmodic thereafter;
flowers usually 3 to 7 per stem, sometimes more; weather
resistance poor; little scent.

Raised by Peter Lambert, Trier, Germany. Introduced 1901.
Parentage: Merveille de Lyon × Caroline Testout. Has been
known also as Snow Queen, Reine des Neiges, White American
Beauty.

FRÜHLINGSGOLD   Cream yellow 7ft shrub

Very vigorous; shrub, upright and arching out as wide as high;
healthy; foliage ample, medium green, matt; flowers creamy
yellow, deep yellow stamens at centre; fading creamy white;
semi-double, with 12 petals, opening to show stamens, up to
4ins diameter; extremely profuse early summer bloom, a
wonderful sight, scarcely any thereafter; flowers on short stalks
borne along side shoots made in former years, arching out from
the plant in an attractive way; weather resistance quite good;
sweet scent.

Raised by Wilhelm Kordes, Sparrieshoop, Germany. Introduced 1937. Parentage: Joanna Hill × *R. spinosissima hispida*.
Also known as Spring Gold.

FRÜHLINGSMORGEN
Pink 5½ft shrub

Fairly vigorous; shrub, upright, spreading out moderately; healthy; foliage ample, dark grey green, not glossy; flowers deep pink with light yellow eye around maroon stamens; fade paler with age; single, with 5 to 7 petals, opening wide to 3½ins diameter, very beautiful; profuse early summer flower, occasional blooms later; flowers on short stalks from wood made in former years; clear and pleasant scent.
Raised by Wilhelm Kordes, Sparrieshoop, Germany. Introduced 1942. Parentage: (E. G. Hill × Catherine Kordes) × R. spinosissima altaica.

GAIL BORDEN
Pink/cream 3ft bush

Vigorous; bush, upright, with good tendency to spread; healthy; foliage abundant, very glossy, dark green; flowers warm salmon inside, yellowish cream outside; slight fading with age; double, very large, with 35 petals, fine cone at centre, opens to 5ins diameter; profuse flower summer and autumn, some between flushes; flowers usually borne one to a stem or 3 to 5; weather resistance very good; scent sweet but light.
Raised by Wilhelm Kordes, Sparrieshoop, Germany. Introduced 1956. Parentage: Mrs Verschuren × Viktoria Adelheid.

GALLICA VERSICOLOR
Striped 2½ft shrub

Vigorous; shrub, upright, dense, compact, many thin shoots; mildew likely; foliage abundant, matt, light green; flowers blush with crimson stripes and marks, a little paler when old, yellow stamens (sometimes light crimson flowers are produced, indicating a reversion to R. gallica officinalis); semi-double, showing stamens, opening flat to 3ins diameter, 18 petals; profuse summer bloom, rarely any thereafter; flowers on shoots growing from old wood, 3 to 7 on a shoot, sometimes produces a large head; weather resistance good; light scent.
Date of discovery unknown; this rose is recorded in literature of the sixteenth century. Parentage: Sport of R. gallica officinalis. Also known as Rosa Mundi, and (incorrectly) as 'York and Lancaster'.

GENERAL MacARTHUR   Crimson 3ft bush

Vigorous; bush, upright and spreading well; healthy; foliage abundant, matt, medium green; flowers bright pale crimson, slightly more purple with age; double, with 35 petals, well formed but loose centre, soon parting, opens to 4ins diameter; profuse summer and autumn bloom, good continuity of spasmodic flower between flushes; flowers 1 to 3 per stem, sometimes more; weather resistance good; rich lemon scent.
Raised by E. G. Hill Co., Richmond, Indiana, USA. Introduced 1905. Parentage; Unknown.

GLORY OF CEYLON   Tea yellow 3ft bush

Vigorous; bush, upright with strong stiff stems, spreading moderately; healthy; foliage ample, glossy, dark green; flowers open dusky tea yellow with red marks, fade yellow, pale when old; semi-double, with 14 petals, open cupped to show stamens, 3½ins diameter; free flowering summer and autumn, good succession between flushes; flowers in large heads, or 3 to 7 on side shoots; weather resistance fair; strong sweet scent.
Raised by R. Harkness & Co. Ltd, Hitchin, Hertfordshire. Introduced 1967. Parentage: Vera Dalton × Masquerade.

GOLD CROWN   Yellow 4ft bush

Vigorous; bush, upright, spreading moderately; slight mildew; foliage ample, very glossy, bright deep green; flowers strong yellow, pink tinges on outer petals, do not fade much; double, large, with 38 veined petals, well formed cone at centre, opening 5½ins diameter; profuse summer and autumn bloom, some between flushes; flowers usually 1 to 3 per stem, sometimes more; early shoots sometimes blind; weather resistance fair; light but sweet scent.
Raised by Reimer Kordes, Sparrieshoop, Germany. Introduced 1959. Parentage: Peace × Spek's Yellow. Name is translated from the original Gold Krone.

GOLDEN MELODY   Pale yellow 2½ft bush

Vigorous; bush, upright, spreading out well; slight mildew; foliage moderately abundant, semi-glossy, deep green; flowers warm pale yellow, sometimes with flush of pinky buff; fade

cream with age; double, 24 large petals, well formed cone at centre, diameter 4½ins; free summer and autumn bloom, some between flushes; flowers borne 1 to 5 per stem, just occasionally in a large head; weather resistance fair; rich lemon scent.
Raised by La Florida, Bilbao, Spain. Introduced 1934. Parentage: Mme Butterfly × (Lady Hillingdon × Souvenir de Claudius Pernet). The proper name is Irene Churruca.

GOLDEN SHOWERS   Yellow 6ft climber

Vigorous; climber, in reality a tall upright bush which lends itself to be treated as a moderate growing climber, or as a hedge in which the longer shoots need support; healthy; foliage abundant, very glossy, bright deep green; flowers strong yellow, opening to show dark stamens, fading paler; semi-double, with 20 petals, well formed centre when young, soon opening wide; very free flowering summer and autumn, usually has some colour on it between flushes; flowers 3 to 5 per stem, sometimes in large heads; weather resistance good; faint scent.
Raised by Dr W. E. Lammerts, Livermore, California, USA. Introduced 1957. Parentage: Charlotte Armstrong × Capt. Thomas.

GOLDEN WINGS   Yellow 4½ft shrub

Vigorous; shrub, stems apart giving open appearance, spreading as wide as high; healthy; foliage ample, large, semi-glossy, middle green; flowers light yellow, showing amber-red stamens, paler with age; single, with 5 to 8 petals, opening wide to 4ins diameter; free flowering in summer and repeats spasmodically to autumn; flowers in groups of about 7 close together, often on rather lax side shoots, sometimes in larger heads on main shoots; weather resistance fair; scent musky.
Raised by R. & A. Shepherd, Medina, Ohio, USA. Introduced 1956. Parentage: Soeur Thérèse × (*R. spinosissima altaica* × Ormiston Roy).

GOLDGLEAM   Yellow 2ft bush

Vigorous; bush, short spreading growth; healthy; foliage ample, glossy, dark green; flowers bright yellow, fade little; semi-double, with 22 petals, holding good cone at centre, finally opening 3½ins diameter; profuse bloom summer and autumn, some between flushes; flowers in clusters of 3 to 5, sometimes singly, occasionally in larger heads; weather resistance very good; light but sweet scent.

Raised by E. B. le Grice, North Walsham, Norfolk. Introduced 1966. Parentage: Gleaming × Allgold.

GRAND'MÈRE JENNY   Yellow/pink 2½ft bush

Moderately vigorous; bush, decidedly upright in habit, spreads out neatly; some blackspot; foliage moderately abundant, glossy, dark green, handsome; flowers basically yellowish cream, tinges of pink on outsides of petals, peach in centre, fading a little with age; double, with 32 petals, extremely well formed cone at centre, opening fairly soon to 4½ins diameter; very abundant flower in summer and autumn, some between flushes; flowers singly or several to a stem, seems to get a flower on every little shoot it possibly can; weather resistance good; scent sweet.

Raised by Francis Meilland, Cap d'Antibes, France. Introduced 1950. Parentage: Peace × (Julien Potin × Sensation).

GRANDPA DICKSON   Yellow 3ft bush

Vigorous; bush, upright and spreading well; healthy; foliage abundant, fairly glossy, light green; flowers light yellow with greenish tinge, fading creamy with age; double, large, with 35 petals, forming very shapely cone at centre (occasionally split), opening to 5ins diameter; abundant bloom summer and autumn, also between flushes; flowers in large heads on main shoots, singly or few to side shoots; weather resistance good; faint scent.

Raised by Patrick Dickson, Newtownards, Northern Ireland. Introduced 1966. Parentage: (Perfecta × Governador Braga da Cruz) × Piccadilly.

GUINEVERE   Pink 2½ft bush

Vigorous; bush, upright, spreading out in a handsome way; slight mildew; foliage very abundant, deep green, matt; flowers rose pink, with a slight apricot flush right at the base, fading a little with age; double, large, with 40 petals, rather rounded flower with fine straight centre, opening 4ins diameter; very abundant flower summer and autumn, with quite a few

between flushes; flowers frequently one to a stem, sometimes 3, occasionally produces a large head of flower; weather resistance good; slight scent.
Raised by R. Harkness & Co. Ltd, Hitchin, Hertfordshire. Introduced 1967. Parentage: Red Dandy × Peace.

GUSTAV FRAHM   Bright crimson 3ft bush

Vigorous; bush, upright, restrained lateral spread, strong upstanding plant; healthy; foliage abundant, glossy, light green; flowers bright dark crimson, losing brightness with age; flowers double, with 25 rather wavy petals, opening flat, rosette formation, about 2½ins diameter; very abundant summer and autumn flower, some between flushes; flowers in large heads; weather resistance fairly good; faint scent.
Raised by Wilhelm Kordes, Sparrieshoop, Germany. Introduced 1958. Parentage: Fanal × Ama.

HEIDELBERG   Crimson 5ft shrub

Vigorous; shrub, upright with moderate lateral spread; healthy; foliage very abundant, glossy, dark green, handsome; flowers rich crimson, a little paler with age; semi-double, with 28 petals, loose centre soon opening from attractive young stage to 3½ins diameter; profuse summer and autumn flower, some between flushes; flowers 1 to 3 per stem, sometimes in larger heads; weather resistance good; faint scent.
Raised by Reimer Kordes, Sparrieshoop, Germany. Introduced 1959. Parentage: Minna Kordes × Floradora.

HELEN TRAUBEL   Peach pink 3ft bush

Vigorous; bush, upright with ready lateral spread; some mildew; foliage abundant, semi-glossy, dark green, copper green when young; flowers warm peach pink, yellow flush at base, fading slightly with age; double, with 28 petals, attractive form young, soon opening wide to 4½ins diameter; very free flowering in summer and autumn, some between flushes; flowers normally 3 to a stem, some tendency to droop a little; weather resistance fairly good; sweet scent.
Raised by H. C. Swim for Armstrong Nurseries, Ontario, California, USA. Introduced 1951. Parentage: Charlotte Armstrong × Glowing Sunset.

HERSELF　　　　　　　　　　　Pearl pink 2ft bush

Moderately vigorous; bush, upright, spreading out well; healthy; foliage fairly abundant, semi-glossy, dark green; flowers warm pale pink lightening to pearl with age; double, with 33 petals regularly arranged, showing stamens, opening to 3½ins diameter; profuse summer and autumn flower, some between flushes; flowers in heads of many blooms, well spaced; weather resistance good; sweet scent.
Raised by G. C. Vincent, Hemingford Grey, Huntingdon. Introduced 1965. Parentage: Sweet Repose × Ma Perkins.

ICEBERG　　　　　　　　　　　　　White 3ft bush

Very vigorous; bush, upright with slender shoots, spreading into very shapely, rounded, plant; slight blackspot; foliage very abundant, glossy, light green, leaves pointed; flowers pure white, sometimes flushed pale pink, developing pink spots with age; semi-double, with 32 petals, pretty centre when young, opening flat to 3ins diameter; extremely profuse, with three abundant flushes and some flower between; flowers in clusters usually of 7, but may also produce large heads, and has excellent habit of flowering down the sides of the bush; weather resistance excellent; slight pleasant scent.
Raised by Reimer Kordes, Sparrieshoop, Germany. Introduced 1958. Parentage: Robin Hood × Virgo. The original name is Schneewittchen, the French name Fée des Neiges.

INNOCENCE　　　　　　　　　　　White 3ft bush

Vigorous; bush, decidedly upright; healthy; foliage abundant, semi-glossy, middle green; flowers white, tinged cream, a few pink flecks, showing beautiful red stamens; single, with 7 petals, opening wide to 4½ins diameter; free flowering summer and autumn, some between; flowers usually produced in large heads, sometimes 3 to a shoot; weather resistance fairly good; sweet scent.
Raised by Chaplin Bros Ltd, Waltham Cross, Hertfordshire. Introduced 1921. Parentage: Unknown.

ISOBEL HARKNESS　　　　　　　　Yellow 2½ft bush

Vigorous; bush, upright growth, spreading out well; some blackspot; foliage ample, glossy, bright medium green; flowers bright yellow, a little paler when old; double, with 30 petals, good straight centre soon opening to 5ins diameter; very free flowering summer and autumn, some between; flowers usually 1 to 3 per stem; weather resistance good; sweet, light, scent. Raised by Albert Norman, Normandy, Surrey. Introduced 1957. Parentage: McGredy's Yellow × Phyllis Gold.

JOSEPHINE BRUCE   Crimson 2ft bush

Vigorous; bush, spreading wider than high; some mildew; foliage ample, dull, middle green; flowers bright crimson, very glowing, dark colour, fades with black tinges; double, with 25 petals, well formed cone at centre, large velvety petals, opening to 5ins diameter; free flowering summer and autumn, some between flushes; flowers borne singly, or 3 to a stem, occasionally in a large head; weather resistance fair; rich, lemon scent. Raised by Bees Ltd, Chester. Introduced 1949. Parentage: Crimson Glory × Madge Whipp, according to the records, but I am told it may have been Crimson Glory × Jane Thornton.

JOSEPH'S COAT   Yellow/red 5ft shrub

Very vigorous; shrub, with long, strong stems, forming stout upright bush, has also been used as climber, but not easy to train that way; healthy; foliage abundant, glossy, large, bright middle green; flowers yellowish orange flushed carmine to scarlet, very bright, fading pinker; semi-double, loosely formed flower of 15 petals opening to 3ins diameter; extremely prolific summer bloom, autumn flush not quite so free, some between flushes; flowers in large heads on straight stems, a spectacular plant; weather resistance fair; sweet if light scent. Raised by David Armstrong and H. C. Swim, Ontario, California, USA. Introduced 1964. Parentage: Buccaneer × Circus.

JOVE   Scarlet 2ft bush

Vigorous; bush, upright growth, spreading well in proportion; very healthy; foliage abundant, very glossy dark green; flowers brilliant scarlet, turning crimson with age, long lasting; semi-double, with 10 petals, waved, opening to show stamens soon;

diameter 2½ins; very free flowering summer and autumn, generous amount between flushes; flowers in large heads, very evenly arranged; weather resistance excellent; faint scent. Raised by R. Harkness & Co. Ltd, Hitchin, Hertfordshire. Introduced 1968. Parentage: Vera Dalton × Paprika.

KÄTHE DUVIGNEAU   Crimson 2½ft bush

Vigorous; bush, upright growth spreading out readily; very healthy; foliage abundant, glossy, middle green with coppery tinge; flowers bright crimson scarlet, more crimson with age; semi-double, opening to 2½ins diameter, with 16 petals; profuse summer and autumn flower, some between flushes; flowers usually 5 to a stem or in large heads; weather resistance good; faint, sweet scent. Raised by Mathias Tantau, Uetersen, Germany. Introduced 1942. Parentage: Baby Château × *R. roxburghii*.

KING ARTHUR   Salmon pink 3½ft bush

Very vigorous; bush, upright, spreading almost as wide as high; healthy; foliage very abundant, large, close set, glossy deep green, purple tinge when young; flowers clear salmon pink, do not fade much; double, opening to 3½ins diameter, with 32 petals, fine straight centre; extremely abundant flower, very quick to repeat, should give three major flushes in the season with some in between; flowers in heads of 5 to many, or on side shoots of 1 to 3 per shoot; weather resistance good apart from red spots induced by rain; slight scent. Raised by R. Harkness & Co. Ltd, Hitchin, Hertfordshire. Introduced 1967. Parentage: Pink Parfait × Highlight.

KING'S RANSOM   Yellow 3ft bush

Vigorous; bush, upright, spreading slightly to make handsome plant; slight mildew; foliage abundant, very glossy, large, handsome, bright green; flowers clear yellow, fading to primrose yellow; double, opening to 4ins diameter, with 35 petals; closed, attractive centre; profuse bloom summer and autumn, some between flushes; flowers borne 1 to 3 on a stem, sometimes more; weather resistance fair; light but sweet scent. Raised by Dennison Morey, Santa Rosa, California, USA. Introduced 1961. Parentage: Golden Masterpiece × Lydia.

LADY HILLINGDON   Yellow 2ft bush

Not vigorous; bush, with thin pendulous branches, open
appearance; healthy; foliage rather sparse, bronze green,
slightly glossy; flowers yellow, with tendency towards apricot,
fascinating colour, fading lighter with age; semi-double, but of
fine high-centred form while young, opening to 4ins diameter,
with about 18 petals; flowers spasmodically, rarely many out at
a time, but continuous summer to autumn; usually carries up to
5 flowers on a stem, opening one or two at a time; weather
resistance good; sweet spicy scent.
Raised by Lowe & Shawyer, Uxbridge, Middlesex. Introduced
1910. Parentage: Papa Gontier × Mme Hoste.

LADY SYLVIA   Pink 3ft bush

Vigorous; bush, upright, spreading to make shapely upright
plant; healthy; foliage moderately abundant, matt, middle to
deep green; flowers light rose pink with deep rose flushes,
fading lighter; double, opening to 3½ins diameter, with 28
petals, well formed straight centre; free flowering summer and
autumn, plenty of flowers between flushes; flowers borne usually 3 or 5 to a stem, sometimes in large heads; weather resistance good; rich lemon scent.
Discovered by Walter Stevens, Hoddesdon, Hertfordshire.
Introduced 1926. Parentage: Sport of Mme Butterfly.

LA JOLLA   Peach/yellow 2½ft bush

Moderately vigorous; bush, upright, spreading out from the
upper half; slight mildew; foliage fairly abundant, pointed
leaves, glossy, dark green; flowers pink in bud, open carmine
pink on pale peach yellow at base; in hot weather colour is pale
peach yellow; old flowers paler in each case; double, opening
to 5ins diameter, with 40 petals and beautiful straight centre;
free flowering, usually gives a superb display on first flush,
thereafter apt to be disappointing in quality until the autumn;
flowers singly, or 3 to 5 to a stem; stems tend to be pendulous;
weather resistance very good; light scent, not sweet.
Raised by H. C. Swim for Armstrong Nurseries, Ontario,
California, USA. Introduced 1954. Parentage: Charlotte
Armstrong × Contrast.

LÉONTINE GERVAIS   Peach pink 12ft climber

Vigorous; climber, with rather pendulous shoots; easy to train;
healthy; foliage abundant, glossy, bright green; flowers pale
peach pink, becoming lighter with age; semi-double, opening to
2ins diameter, with 20 petals, soon showing centre; profuse
summer flush, hardly any flowers thereafter; flowers on side
shoots growing from the wood of former years; often singly,
sometimes 3 to a shoot, not often many more; flowers are thus
well spaced on the plant with the bright foliage showing
between them; weather resistance fair; faint scent.
Raised by Barbier & Co., Orléans, France. Introduced 1903.
Parentage: *R. wichuraiana* × Souvenir de Catherine Guillot.

LILLI MARLENE   Crimson 2½ft bush

Vigorous; bush, with dense compact growth, upright; some
mildew; foliage abundant, deep green, semi-glossy; flowers
bright crimson, with sparkling sheen, showing stamens, more
dull with age; semi-double, opening 2½ins diameter, with 24
petals, rather cupped shape; very profuse in bloom summer
and autumn, with some between flushes; flowers borne in
heads, sometimes of many, more often of about 7 flowers
together; weather resistance quite good; slight scent.
Raised by Reimer Kordes, Sparrieshoop, Germany. Introduced
1959. Parentage: (Our Princess × Rudolf Timm) × Ama.

LITTLE LADY   White 1½ft bush

Vigorous; bush, low growing, neat, spreading well; healthy;
foliage ample, narrow leaves, pointed, slightly bluish green,
glossy; flowers white, sometimes blush, with slight mauve-pink
flushes on outer petals; double, opening to 2ins diameter, with
70 tiny petals arranged crinoline fashion around the centre;
free flowering summer and autumn, not many between flushes;
flowers in little heads of 3 to 7, sometimes in larger heads;
weather resistance quite good; faint scent.
Raised by R. Harkness & Co. Ltd, Hitchin, Hertfordshire.
Introduced 1967. Parentage: Iceberg × Baby Faurax.

LITTLE WHITE PET White 1½ft bush

Moderately vigorous; bush, short, spreading, well filled in; healthy; foliage moderately abundant, small, matt, dark greyish green; flowers from red buds opening slightly blush, usually white when full out with pink flushes on outer petals; double, opening to 1½ins diameter, with 60 small petals lying flat around the centre in very attractive formation; profuse summer flush, after which there are usually a few flowers on the plant right through to late autumn; flowers in heads with many flowers, or about 3 to 5 on the smaller shoots; weather resistance fair; light scent.
Raised by P. Henderson, New York, USA. Introduced 1879. Parentage: In doubt, said to be a sport from Félicité et Perpétue.

LORD PENZANCE Pink/yellow 6ft shrub

Vigorous; shrub, spreading as wide as high; healthy; foliage small, semi-glossy, dark green; the sweet briar scent of the foliage is the prime reason for growing Lord Penzance; flowers pink and yellow, fleeting; single, opening to 1 inch with 5 petals; moderate amount of flowers in summer, usually none thereafter; borne on side shoots arising from old wood; weather resistance fair; slight flower scent, but the scent of the foliage spreads over the garden on a summer evening.
Raised by Lord Penzance. Introduced 1894. Parentage: *R. rubiginosa* × Harison's Yellow.

LUCY CRAMPHORN Carmine scarlet 3½ft bush

Vigorous; bush, upright, spreading out strongly; healthy; foliage abundant, glossy, dark green with coppery tinge; flowers bright carmine scarlet, going a little towards crimson purple with age; double, opening to 5ins diameter, with tight cone at centre, 35 petals; free flowering summer and autumn, some between flushes; flowers usually 3 to a stem, good long stems; weather resistance fair; scent light and sweet.
Raised by Michel Kriloff, Antibes, France. Introduced 1960. Parentage: Peace × Baccara. Original name is Maryse Kriloff.

MAGENTA Greyish magenta 4ft shrub

Very vigorous; shrub, with upright pliant shoots, forming a bush not quite as wide as high; healthy; foliage abundant, semi-glossy, medium to deep green; flowers greyish magenta rose, deep colour on opening, becoming lighter; double, opening 3ins diameter, quite flat, with 50 petals, sometimes showing quartered centre; very profuse bloom summer and autumn, some between flushes; usually flowers in very large heads; weather resistance fair; spicy scent.

Raised by Wilhelm Kordes, Sparrieshoop, Germany. Introduced 1954. Parentage: Seedling × Lavender Pinocchio.

MAIDEN'S BLUSH   Blush 5ft shrub

Very vigorous; shrub, upright, and spreading to form a wide upright plant; healthy; foliage very abundant, matt, greyish green; flowers blush, fading white; semi-double, opening to 2½ins diameter, quite flat, petals irregularly placed; profuse summer flush, scarcely any thereafter; flowers on side shoots growing from wood of previous years; weather resistance fairly good; sweet scent.

Origin unknown, thought to be a natural hybrid, and recorded in the 1500's. Two forms are grown, Maiden's Blush Great and Small, the latter rather lower growing, noted at Kew Gardens in 1797.

MAIGOLD   Peachy yellow 20ft climber

Very vigorous; climber, with strong shoots bearing many bristly thorns, easy to train, needs adequate space; very healthy; foliage abundant, close set, large, glossy, handsome, bright middle green; flowers peachy yellow, not fading much; semi-double, opening to 3½ins diameter, soon showing centre, 15 petals; very abundant flush in early summer, scattered flower thereafter; flowers on side shoots growing from wood of former years, 1 to 5 per stem; weather resistance fairly good; unusual scent, strong.

Raised by Wilhelm Kordes, Sparrieshoop, Germany. Introduced 1953. Parentage: Poulsen's Pink × Frühlingstag.

MANX QUEEN   Orange/pink 2½ft bush

Vigorous; bush, upright and spreading wide; healthy; foliage abundant, glossy, middle green; flowers orange at centre, deep carmine towards top petal edges, fading yellow and pink; semi-double, opening to 3½ins diameter, with 24 petals, soon showing

open centre; very abundant flower summer and autumn, some
between flushes; flowers in clusters of 3 to 6, sometimes in
large heads; weather resistance fair; light scent.
Raised by Patrick Dickson, Newtownards, Northern Ireland.
Introduced 1963. Parentage: Shepherd's Delight × Circus.
Also known as Isle of Man.

MARY WALLACE   Pink 12ft climber

Vigorous; climber, fairly tidy growth, easy to train; healthy;
foliage ample, glossy, medium to light green; flowers rose pink,
fading a little paler when old; semi-double, opening to 4ins
diameter, with about 20 petals, forming good centre in young
stages; prolific summer flush, scarcely any thereafter; flowers
in clusters of 3 to 7 on side shoots growing from wood made in
former years; weather resistance good; scent sweet.
Raised by Dr Walter van Fleet, Glenn Dale, Maryland, USA.
Introduced 1924. Parentage: *R. wichuraiana* × unknown pink
H.T.

MATTERHORN   Cream white 4ft bush

Very vigorous; bush, upright, with strong shoots, spreading
into stout bush; healthy; foliage abundant, semi-glossy, large,
middle green; flowers very pale lemon on opening, soon turning
creamy white; semi-double, opening to 3½ins diameter, with
attractive straight centre while young; prolific summer and
autumn bloom, some between flushes; flowers in heads, quite
close together, usually 5 to 12, occasionally many per stem;
weather resistance fair; sweet light scent.
Raised by David Armstrong and H. C. Swim, Ontario, California, USA. Introduced 1965. Parentage: Buccaneer × Cherry
Glow.

MAY QUEEN   Pink 15ft climber

Vigorous; climber, stems not too stiff, easy to train; healthy;
foliage abundant, glossy, deep green; flowers rose pink, a
lively colour, not fading much; double, opening to 2½ins
diameter, with about 35 petals, centre usually quartered,
attractive; very profuse summer flush, with occasional scattered
flower thereafter; flowers on side shoots produced from wood of

former years, usually 1 to 3 to a stem, occasionally more; weather resistance good; sweet fruity scent.

Origin uncertain; introduced in America in 1898.

MEG   Peach pink 15ft climber

Vigorous; climber, rather stiff shoots, quick growing; healthy; foliage abundant, semi-glossy, medium green; flowers open from red buds to reddish peach, fading peach pink; semi-double, opening to $3\frac{1}{2}$ins diameter, with 10 large petals, often scalloped at edges, showing stamens soon; prolific summer flower, quite a few in autumn too, not many between flushes; flowers on side shoots from wood made in former years, usually 1 to 5 per stem, occasionally in a large head; weather resistance fairly good; sweet scent.

Raised by Dr A. C. V. Gosset, Liphook, Hampshire. Introduced 1954. Parentage: Thought to be Paul's Lemon Pillar × Mme Butterfly.

MERLIN   Pink/yellow 2ft bush

Vigorous; bush, upright, maintains neat and compact shape; foliage ample, deep green, glossy; flowers open from red buds, reddish pink with yellow at base, very gay, fading reddish pink with age; semi-double, opening to 3ins diameter, with 22 petals, holding closed centre, which often has a twist in it, until flowers well developed; very abundant summer and autumn flower, good number between flushes; flowers in large heads, or on side shoots with 1 to 5 per stem; weather resistance good; slight scent.

Raised by R. Harkness & Co. Ltd, Hitchin, Hertfordshire. Introduced 1967. Parentage: Pink Parfait × Circus.

MERMAID   Cream yellow 15ft climber

Vigorous; climber, with stiff shoots, brittle, and difficult to train as they break easily; usually slow to establish itself; healthy, but not perfectly hardy; foliage abundant, glossy, dark green, stays on late, quite individual; flowers open pale yellow, immediately showing rich cluster of bright stamens, creating a deep yellow centre; fading paler with age; single, wide open flower to $4\frac{1}{2}$ins diameter, with 5 large petals; flowers freely in summer, and continues to show flowers in lesser profusion until

late autumn; flowers borne on side shoots produced from wood of former years, including very old wood, and, more rarely, on new basal shoots; usually 3 to 15 per stem, but occasionally singly or many; weather resistance fair; scent sweet.
Raised by William Paul & Son, Waltham Cross, Hertfordshire. Introduced 1918. Parentage: *R. bracteata* × yellow tea rose.

MICHÉLE MEILLAND   Peach pink 2½ft bush

Moderately vigorous; bush, upright with slender, spreading top growth; healthy; foliage fairly abundant, semi-glossy, medium to deep green; flowers light pink, peach deep in centre, the peach colour or the pink predominate at different seasons; fading paler with age; double, opening to 4ins diameter, with 24 petals, attractive form when young with cone at centre; profuse summer and autumn flower, quite a few between flushes; flowers usually 3 or 4 to a stem, sometimes many, the stems long and graceful; weather resistance good; sweet scent.
Raised by Francis Meilland, Cap d'Antibes, France. Introduced 1945. Parentage: Joanna Hill × Peace.

MILORD   Crimson 2½ft bush

Vigorous; bush, upright, spreading out to good proportions; healthy; foliage abundant, dull, middle green with copper tinge early; flowers crimson scarlet, not fading much; double, opening to 4½ins diameter, well formed but soon opening; free flowering summer and autumn, some between flushes; flowers borne singly or more often 3 to 5 per stem; weather resistance good; sweet if light scent.
Raised by Sam McGredy, Portadown, Northern Ireland. Introduced 1962. Parentage: Rubaiyat × Karl Herbst.

MISCHIEF   Salmon 3ft bush

Very vigorous; bush, spreading as wide as high, very well filled; some rust; foliage abundant, semi-glossy, dark green; flowers open strong deep reddish pink, develop to salmon; double, opening to 4½ins diameter, with 32 petals, well formed cone at centre; very prolific summer and autumn flower, good allowance in between flushes; flowers borne 1 to 3 per stem, occasionally more; weather resistance good; sweet scent.
Raised by Sam McGredy, Portadown, Northern Ireland. Introduced 1960. Parentage: Peace × Spartan.

Mme BUTTERFLY   Light pink 3ft bush

This rose is exactly the same as Lady Sylvia, except for the colour: flowers light rose pink with yellow at base of petals; fading light blush.

Discovered by E. G. Hill Co., Richmond, Indiana, USA. Introduced 1918. Parentage: Sport of Ophelia.

Mme GRÉGOIRE STAECHELIN   Pink 15ft climber

Vigorous; climber, with fairly stiff stems, easy to train; healthy; foliage abundant, semi-glossy, medium to deep green; flowers warm rose pink, slightly paler when old, red flushes on outside; semi-double, opening to 4½ins diameter, about 15 large ruffled petals; extremely profuse early summer flower, hardly any thereafter; flowers borne on side shoots from wood of former years, usually 3 to 5 per stem; weather resistance good; scent sweet and rich.

Raised by Pedro Dot, Barcelona, Spain. Introduced 1927. Parentage: Frau Karl Druschki × Château de Clos Vougeot. Also known as Spanish Beauty.

Mme HARDY   White 5ft shrub

Vigorous; shrub, growing upright and spreading out to make a wide, predominantly upright plant; some mildew; foliage moderately abundant, matt, middle to light green; flowers white, with slight pink blush, particularly at outer petals, not fading much; double, opening to 4ins diameter, with a great many petals (I never counted them, probably over 60); the flowers are often quartered, and the petals arranged in a charming way around the centre, which shows green; free summer flower, hardly any thereafter; flowers on side shoots, often long, growing from wood made in former years; usually 1 to 5 per shoot, occasionally more; weather resistance small; sweet scent.

Raised by M. Hardy, Paris, France. Introduced 1832. Parentage: Unknown.

MOJAVE   Orange red 3ft bush

Vigorous; bush, decidedly upright, makes a good plant; foliage abundant, glossy, dark green; healthy; flowers red orange in

bud, opening bright pink orange with red flecks, fading more
pink; semi-double, opening to 4ins diameter, with 20 petals,
very attractive young flower, opening rather quickly; flowers
very freely summer and autumn, with some between flushes;
often bears blooms singly on straight firm stems, also 3 or 5 per
stem; weather resistance fairly good; mild sweet scent.
Raised by H. C. Swim for Armstrong Nurseries, Ontario,
California, USA. Introduced 1954. Parentage: Charlotte
Armstrong × Signora.

MONTEZUMA   Salmon 3½ft bush

Very vigorous; bush, upright with free growth, willing to form
wide plant; very healthy; foliage abundant, large, semi-glossy,
deep green; flowers pale crimson in bud, opening deep salmon,
fading pinker with purplish tinges; double, opening to 4ins
diameter, with 24 petals; firm, straight and attractive centre;
profuse summer and autumn flower, good continuity between
main flushes; flowers usually borne 3 to 5 per stem, sometimes
more; weather resistance poor; faint scent.
Raised by H. C. Swim for Armstrong Nurseries, Ontario,
California, USA. Introduced 1955. Parentage: Fandango ×
Floradora.

MOONRAKER   Cream 3½ft bush

Very vigorous; bush, upright, and spreading bold and wide;
healthy; foliage very abundant, semi-glossy, deep green, filling
the plant well; flowers open ivory with gold at base, fade creamy
white; semi-double, 3½ins diameter, with 30 petals, slightly
twisted centre, opening wide; extremely profuse in flower
summer and autumn, giving three good flushes with generous
amount between; flowers borne in large heads, or frequently
3 to 5 on side shoots; weather resistance very good; slight scent.
Raised by R. Harkness & Co. Ltd, Hitchin, Hertfordshire.
Introduced 1968. Parentage: Pink Parfait × Highlight.

MOYESII   Crimson 9ft shrub

Vigorous; shrub, very upright, main shoots tall, apart, arching
slightly, with thin side shoots; healthy; foliage sparse, with 7
to 13 leaflets to each leaf, light to middle green, gives plant
light and airy appearance: flowers vivid crimson, showing

yellow stamens, do not stay on long enough to fade very much; single, about 2ins diameter, with 5 petals, very memorable; flowers scattered about bush in summer, none thereafter, but the long flask-shaped scarlet heps in the autumn are very beautiful indeed; flowers on short stalks near the tips of side shoots growing from old wood; weather resistance fair; little scent. Wild rose introduced from North-west China, 1894.

Mrs JOHN LAING   Pink 4ft bush

Vigorous; bush, upright, spreading moderately; some mildew; foliage ample, matt, light green; flowers soft rose pink, bright, not fading much; double, opening to 4½ins diameter, with 44 petals, very beautiful rounded shape with closed, symmetrical centre; free flowering in the summer, occasional flowers only thereafter; often bears flowers one to a stem, sometimes more; weather resistance fairly good; sweet scent.
Raised by Henry Bennett, Shepperton, Surrey. Introduced 1887. Parentage: François Michelon × unknown.

Mrs JOSEPH HIESS   Pink 1½ft bush

Vigorous; bush, low spreading growth; healthy; foliage abundant, small, very glossy, dark green; flowers bright rose pink, fading a little with age; double, opening to 2ins diameter, with 38 small petals, no definite symmetry at centre; extremely profuse flower summer and autumn, some between flushes; the summer flush in particular almost covers the bush with flower; flowers usually in large heads, sometimes in clusters of 3 to 9; weather resistance good; light scent.
Raised by R. and A. Shepherd, Medina, Ohio, USA. Introduced 1943. Parentage: Roserie × unknown.

MY CHOICE   Pink/yellow 2½ft bush

Vigorous; bush, upright and spreading well; healthy; foliage abundant, semi-glossy, dark green; flowers carmine to salmon pink inside, pale cream outside, with yellow in the centre; fading a little with age; double, opening to 5ins diameter, with 37 petals, a large and beautifully formed flower, good cone at centre; very free summer and autumn flower, some between flushes; flowers often borne singly, or 3 to a stem, rarely more; weather resistance good; rich lemon scent.

Raised by E. B. le Grice, North Walsham, Norfolk. Introduced 1959. Parentage: Wellworth × Ena Harkness.

NATHALIE NYPELS   Pink 2½ft bush

Vigorous; bush, spreading out readily as wide as high; some mildew; foliage abundant, small and pointed, glossy, dark green; flowers light rose pink, fading almost white when old; semi-double, opening to 2½ins diameter, with 20 petals, rather loose formation; extremely profuse bloom summer to autumn, with some between flushes; flowers borne in large heads; weather resistance good; sweet scent.
Raised by M. Leenders & Co., Tegelen, Holland. Introduced 1919. Parentage: Orléans Rose × (Comtesse du Cayla × Austrian Copper).

NEVADA   White 6ft shrub

Very vigorous; shrub, with arching branches, spreading out as wide as high; some blackspot; foliage abundant, small, soft, light green; flowers white, with yellow centre; sometimes the later flowers are flushed pink; semi-double, opening to 3½ins diameter, showing stamens, general effect of a single rose, though Nevada has about 8 petals; flowers in fantastic profusion early summer, almost hiding foliage, and after a month or so to rest produces quite a good few flowers late summer and autumn; the flowers grow on short stems from side shoots arising along the wood made in former years, also at the ends of new main and side shoots; weather resistance fairly good; slight musky scent.
Raised by Pedro Dot, Barcelona, Spain. Introduced 1927. Parentage: La Giralda × *R. moyesii*.

NEW DAWN   Blush 5ft shrub

Very vigorous; shrub, with long shoots growing outwards, allowing the plant to grow considerably wider than high; it may also be trained as a climber; healthy; foliage abundant, rather small, bright middle green, very glossy; flowers light blush pink, not fading much; semi-double, opening to 3ins diameter, with 24 petals, most attractive straight centre when young, eventually opening wide; extremely free flowering in summer, rather variable amount of subsequent bloom to autumn;

flowers in very large heads, and often on long shoots of 3 to 12 blooms; weather resistance good; sweet rich scent.

Discovered by Somerset Rose Nurseries, New Brunswick, New Jersey, USA. Introduced 1930. Parentage: Sport of Dr W. van Fleet, which it resembles exactly in flower and foliage.

OLALA   Crimson 2½ft bush

Very vigorous; bush, upright and spreading out to make a fine, strong plant; healthy; foliage abundant, large, dark green, glossy; flowers bright crimson, lighter in centre, not fading much; semi-double, opening about 3ins diameter, with 18 petals, showing centre soon; very abundant flower summer and autumn, with some between flushes; flowers in large heads, occasionally in clusters of 3 to 7; weather resistance good; faint scent.

Raised by Mathias Tantau, Uetersen, Germany. Introduced 1956. Parentage: Fanal × Crimson Glory.

OLÉ   Scarlet 2½ft bush

Moderately vigorous; bush, rather upright, spreading moderately; some mosaic virus; foliage ample, very glossy, middle green; flowers strong scarlet, not fading much; double, opening to 4ins diameter, with 35 petals, often scalloped at edges, tightly packed in well formed flower; free summer and autumn flower, some between flushes; flowers usually 3 to 5 to a stem, but sometimes in large heads; weather resistance good; light, rather bitter scent.

Raised by David Armstrong, Ontario, California, USA. Introduced 1964. Parentage: Roundelay × El Capitan.

OPHELIA   Light blush 3ft bush

This rose is exactly the same as Lady Sylvia, except for the colour and scent: flowers very pale blush with yellow in the deep centre, not fading much; very strong sweet scent.

Raised by William Paul, Waltham Cross, Hertfordshire. Introduced 1912. Parentage: Unknown.

ORANGEADE   Scarlet orange 2½ft bush

Vigorous; bush, spreading freely to form a wide but upright plant: healthy; foliage abundant, glossy dark green, handsome:

flowers vivid scarlet orange, fading a little with age; semi-double, opening to 3½ins diameter, with 12 petals soon showing centre; extremely abundant flower summer and autumn, plenty between flushes; flowers in large heads, or with 3 to 9 to a shoot; weather resistance good; sweet, if light scent.
Raised by Sam McGredy, Portadown, Northern Ireland. Introduced 1959. Parentage: Orange Sweetheart × Independence.

ORANGE SENSATION   Orange scarlet 2ft bush

Vigorous; bush, likes to make many shoots and spread out well; some mildew; foliage abundant, dense, fairly dull, middle green; flowers bright orange scarlet, fading a little with age; semi-double, opening to 2½ins diameter, with 25 petals making delightful neat, straight centre in young stages; very abundant flower summer and autumn, and generous amount between flushes; flowers in large heads, or in groups of 3 to 12 per stem; weather resistance good; sweet scent.
Raised by G. de Ruiter, Hazerswoude, Holland. Introduced 1961. Parentage: Unknown.

ORION   Red 3ft bush

Very vigorous; bush, handsome grower with upright habit spreading out well; very healthy; foliage abundant, large, close set, deep green and glossy; flowers bright light crimson, losing some brightness with age; double, opening to 4½ins diameter, with 30 petals, good cone at centre; very profuse flower summer and autumn, and fine continuity between flushes; flowers in heads of about 9 large flowers, spaced well apart, or sometimes on stems with 3 to 5; weather resistance fairly good; scent light but sweet.
Raised by R. Harkness & Co. Ltd, Hitchin, Hertfordshire. Introduced 1968. Parentage: Pink Parfait × Red Dandy.

PADDY McGREDY   Deep pink 2ft bush

Vigorous; bush, spreading out well and perfectly filled in; some blackspot; foliage abundant, glossy, middle to deep green; flowers deep pink, sometimes flushed salmon red, becoming a little lighter with age; double, opening to 4½ins diameter, with 36 petals, excellent form, attractive cone at

centre in early stages; superbly abundant on its summer flush, when flowers hide the leaves, good in autumn too, but few between flushes; flowers in large heads, or on side shoots with 3 to 5 per stem; weather resistance good; sweet light scent.
Raised by Sam McGredy, Portadown, Northern Ireland. Introduced 1962. Parentage: Spartan × Tzigane.

PAPRIKA   Scarlet 2½ft bush

Vigorous; bush, upright and spreading out freely; healthy; foliage abundant, very shiny, dark green, handsome; flowers bright scarlet, vivid, losing some brightness with age; semi-double, opening to 3½ins diameter, with 14 petals, opening rather crimped to show centres, where stamens are dark, with peppery pollen; extremely profuse summer and autumn flower, some between flushes; flowers well spaced in large heads, or 3 to 9 on side shoots; weather resistance good; faint scent.
Raised by Mathias Tantau, Uetersen, Germany. Introduced 1958. Parentage: Marchenland × Red Favourite.

PARKDIREKTOR RIGGERS   Scarlet 15ft climber

Vigorous; climber, with long shoots, not too stiff for easy training; healthy; foliage abundant, glossy, dark green; flowers bright scarlet crimson, occasionally with central white markings, losing some brightness with age; semi-double, opening to 2½ins diameter, with about 13 petals soon showing centre; very abundant summer flower, with scattered bloom thereafter; flowers on side shoots growing from wood of former years, usually in large clusters; weather resistance good; faint scent.
Raised by Reimer Kordes, Sparrieshoop, Germany. Introduced 1957. Parentage: Kordesii × Our Princess.

PAUL'S SCARLET CLIMBER   Scarlet 12ft climber

Vigorous; climber, with long shoots, easy to train; some mildew; foliage abundant, semi-glossy, medium green; flowers vivid scarlet crimson, turning purple when old; semi-double, opening to 2ins diameter, with about 20 petals, good form when young; very profuse summer bloom, not much afterwards; flowers in heads of many, or in clusters of 3 to 7, on side shoots growing from older wood; weather resistance good; light scent.

Raised by William Paul, Waltham Cross, Hertfordshire. Introduced 1916. Parentage: Unknown.

PEACE   Yellow/pink 3½ft bush

Very vigorous; bush, with strong shoots forming a wide, dense plant; slight mildew and blackspot; foliage abundant, large, glossy, dark green, handsome; flowers yellow with flushes of pink, going pale with age; much variation in the yellow, whether pale or deeper; double, very large, opening to 5ins diameter or more, with about 30 petals forming a rounded flower with straight, beautiful centre; profuse bloom summer and autumn, with some between flushes; flowers are borne singly, or about 3 to a stem, occasionally more, some early shoots may come blind; weather resistance good; scent light but sweet.

Raised by Francis Meilland, Cap d'Antibes, France. Introduced 1942. Parentage: Joanna Hill × ([Charles P. Kilham × Austrian Copper Seedling] × [Charles P. Kilham × Margaret McGredy]). Known also as Mme A. Meilland, Gloria Dei and Gioia.

PENELOPE   Blush 4ft shrub

Very vigorous; shrub, with sturdy shoots growing out to make a wide plant, may remain fairly low for some years; very healthy; foliage abundant, middle green, fairly glossy; flowers creamy blush, sometimes with a slight flush of yellow, fading to a whitish blush; semi-double, opening to about 2½ins diameter, with about 17 petals, showing yellow stamens early; extremely profuse summer flower, but thereafter there is some variation from season to season as to the amount produced to the autumn, most years there will be a reasonable amount of scattered bloom; flowers in very large heads, more rarely in smaller clusters; weather resistance fair; scent sweet and musky.

Raised by the Revd J. H. Pemberton, Havering-atte-Bower, Essex. Introduced 1924. Parentage: Unknown.

PERFECTA   Pink/cream 3ft bush

Vigorous; bush, of upright habit, spreading reasonably well, apt to produce pendulous side shoots; slight blackspot; foliage abundant, dark green, glossy; flowers are variable in colour, the first flush is normally heavily flushed reddish pink on an almost white background, the later flowers having a cream to cream-yellow background with pink flushes; fading lighter with red flecks; very double, opening to 5ins or more diameter, very well formed flowers of about 60 petals, with splendid regular centre, lasting long; very free blooming summer and autumn, with good amount between flushes; flowers usually 3 to 5 per stem, sometimes borne singly, occasionally in heads of 7 or more; the blooms are heavy, weighing some of the more pendulous side shoots down, and suffering the indignity of being snapped off in particularly strong winds; weather resistance fairly good; sweet, light scent.

Raised by Wilhelm Kordes, Sparrieshoop, Germany. Introduced 1957. Parentage: Spek's Yellow × Karl Herbst. The full name is Kordes' Perfecta.

PHYLLIS BIDE   Pink/yellow 7ft climber

Moderately vigorous; climber, restrained growth, may stay bushy; has thin pliable stems strong enough to stand up, easy to train; healthy; a little tender; foliage abundant, small, semi-glossy, lightish green, gives a light, airy impression; flowers pink, with peach to yellow shading within, some pink flecks, fading light pink with age; semi-double, opening to 2ins in diameter, centre soon shown, 20 petals; very profuse flower in summer, with a good repeat in autumn, and some between flushes; most flowers borne in heads of 7 to 12, sometimes singly or few per stem, on side shoots growing from older wood; large heads are borne on new main shoots; weather resistance good; light scent.

Raised by S. Bide & Sons, Farnham, Surrey. Introduced 1923. Parentage: Perle d'Or × Gloire de Dijon.

PICCADILLY   Yellow/red 2½ft bush

Very vigorous; bush, making dense plant with many upright shoots, spreading out into good looking plant; healthy; foliage very abundant, highly glossy, coppery dark green, handsome; flowers yellow to orange yellow, the upper half of the inside petal bright salmon red, veined yellow; colours paler when old; double, opening to 5ins diameter, with 24 large petals forming a fine regular flower with cone at centre; very abundant in flower summer to autumn, may get three flushes in with plenty

between; flowers singly or 3 to 7 per stem, occasionally makes a larger head; weather resistance good; light, sweet scent.
Raised by Sam McGredy, Portadown, Northern Ireland. Introduced 1959. Parentage: McGredy's Yellow × Karl Herbst.

PINK FAVOURITE   Pink 2½ft bush

Vigorous; bush, upright, spreading well, not particularly dense; very healthy; foliage abundant, very highly glossy, bright light green, handsome, covering bush very well; flowers clear deep rose, fading paler with age; double, opening to 5ins diameter, with 24 large petals forming handsome flower with good cone at centre; very abundant summer and autumn flower, some between flushes; flowers usually 3 to 7 per stem, sometimes in larger heads; weather resistance good; scent light but sweet.
Raised by Gordon von Abrams, Davis, California, USA. Introduced 1956. Parentage: Juno × (Georg Arends × New Dawn).

PINK PARFAIT   Pink 2½ft bush

Vigorous; bush, upright, not stiff, spreading out into a plant of gentle, flowing outline; healthy; foliage abundant, matt, middle green; flowers open from carmine buds to light pink, some veining in petals, the shades of pink variable in the flowers and over the season; later blooms have trace of peachy cream; does not fade much; semi-double, opening to 4ins diameter, with 20 petals, extremely beautiful form both while centre closed and after; very prolific, summer to autumn, usually gives 3 main flushes with some between; flowers mainly in heads of several blooms, sometimes 3 per stem, more rarely in large heads; weather resistance good; faint sweet scent.
Raised by H. C. Swim for Armstrong Nurseries, Ontario, California, USA. Introduced 1960. Parentage: First Love × Pinocchio.

PINK PERPÉTUE   Pink 7ft climber

Vigorous; climber, with restrained growth, very easy to train; healthy; foliage ample, medium green, glossy; flowers deep rose pink, often with red flushes outside, do not fade much; double, opening to 3½ins diameter, with 30 petals, good regular centre when young; very free in bloom, summer to autumn, with good succession between flushes; flowers in clusters, usually 3 to 12 per stem, both on side shoots from the older wood, and on new shoots; weather resistance good; sweet scent. Raised by C. Gregory & Sons Ltd, Chilwell, Nottingham. Introduced 1965. Parentage: Danse du Feu × New Dawn.

PRIMA BALLERINA   Pink 3ft bush

Very vigorous; bush, strong upright grower, spreading out to a handsome plant, predominantly upright; very healthy; foliage very abundant, large, slightly glossy, dark coppery green, persistent into winter with purplish colouring; flowers deep pink, a little paler when old; double, opening to 5ins diameter, with 24 large petals, good centre while young, occasionally split; profuse summer and autumn flower, some between flushes; flowers borne singly or 3 to 5 per stem, occasionally more; weather resistance excellent; scent sweet and very rich. Raised by Mathias Tantau, Uetersen, Germany. Introduced 1957. Parentage: Seedling × Peace.

PRINCESS MICHIKO   Orange 2½ft bush

Vigorous; bush, upright, spreading moderately; healthy; foliage abundant, glossy, dark green, handsome; flowers bright orange with yellowish centre; semi-double, opening to 3ins diameter, with 12 petals, soon showing centre; profuse summer and autumn bloom, some between flushes; flowers in clusters of 3 to 9, also in larger heads; weather resistance fair; faint scent. Raised by Patrick Dickson, Newtownards, Northern Ireland. Introduced 1966. Parentage: Spartan × Circus.

QUEEN ELIZABETH   Pink 5ft bush

Very vigorous; bush, decidedly upright, makes so many strong shoots as to thicken it out into a good, substantial plant; healthy; foliage very abundant, glossy, middle green; flowers clear light pink, a little paler with age; double, opening to 3½ins diameter, with 30 petals, good closed, pointed centre while young; very profuse bloom summer and autumn, some between flushes; flowers in well spread heads, usually 4 to 9 per stem, sometimes 1 to 3, sometimes in large heads; weather resistance good; light, agreeable scent.

Raised by Dr W. E. Lammerts, Livermore, California, USA. Introduced 1954. Parentage: Charlotte Armstrong × Floradora.

RED DANDY   Crimson 2½ft bush

Vigorous; bush, upright but spreading easily with rather open habit; healthy; foliage ample, set apart, slightly glossy, middle green; flowers deep scarlet to crimson when old; double, opening to 4ins diameter, with 30 petals, velvety, forming a beautiful closed centre in young stages; free flowering summer to autumn, with many between flushes; flowers often 3 to a stem, but also in larger heads, beautifully arrayed with the flowers well apart; weather resistance good; light, sweet scent. Raised by Albert Norman, Normandy, Surrey. Introduced 1959. Parentage: Ena Harkness × Karl Herbst.

REDGOLD   Yellow/red 3ft bush

Vigorous; bush, upright, with compact outward spread; slight mildew and blackspot; foliage abundant, middle green, slightly glossy; flowers bright yellow edged red; fading orange pink, very gay; semi-double, opening to 3ins diameter, good centre at young stages, 23 petals; very profuse summer and autumn flower, some between flushes; flowers borne well spaced in heads, or 3 to 7 per stem; weather resistance fairly good; scent light but sweet.
Raised by Patrick Dickson, Newtownards, Northern Ireland. Introduced 1966. Parentage: (Karl Herbst × Masquerade) × (Faust × Piccadilly).

RITTER VON BARMSTEDE   Pink 10ft climber

Vigorous; climber, with good number of pliant, easily trained shoots; healthy; foliage moderately abundant, small, glossy, light green; flowers bright deep rose pink; not fading much; semi-double, opening to 2½ins diameter, with 20 petals, centre soon open; very profuse summer flower, with good succession of incidental flowers and a fair flush in autumn; flowers in clusters, usually about 7 to 12 per stem, also in larger heads; borne both on new wood and side shoots from older wood; weather resistance fairly good; sweet scent.
Raised by Wilhelm Kordes, Sparrieshoop, Germany. Intro-

duced 1959. Parentage: Unknown. Note: a light red variety with about 10 petals and small flowers is being sold under this name also.

ROSE GAUJARD   Pink 3ft bush

Very vigorous; bush, upright, spreading to make a large plant; healthy; foliage abundant, very glossy, bright dark green, handsome; flowers carmine pink, flushed on lighter base, turning rose pink inside, always much lighter on outside petals; double, opening to 4½ins diameter, with 45 petals, very fine regular outline, good closed centre, though sometimes split; very free blooming summer and autumn, a good few between flushes; flowers usually 1 to 5 per stem; weather resistance fairly good; faint scent.
Raised by Jean Gaujard, Feysin, Isère, France. Introduced 1957. Parentage: Peace × Opera seedling.

RUBRIFOLIA   Pink 5ft shrub

Vigorous; shrub, spreading as wide as high, or more, with airy, open appearance; healthy; foliage is the great charm of this rose, it is just about ample enough, a lovely greyed red-purple colour, matt; flowers deep rose pink to light red, light at centre, soon fall; single, about 1¼ins diameter, with 5 petals; flowers in summer only, few or none thereafter; borne in close heads of many blooms on side shoots growing from wood of former years; weather resistance fair; light scent; round bright red heps in autumn.
Wild rose from mountainous areas in Central and Southern Europe. Introduced 1830.

RUMBA   Yellow/red 2ft bush

Vigorous; bush, upright, dense, spreading well; some mildew; foliage abundant, glossy, dark yellowish green; flowers extremely varied, bright yellow to orange, rimmed carmine scarlet; or paler yellow and pink; fading pale; double, opening to 1½ins diameter, with 30 petals, open centre surrounded by small, tightly packed petals; very profuse in summer and autumn with some between flushes; flowers in large heads, the flowers close together; weather resistance good; scent faint but sweet.

Raised by Svend Poulsen, Copenhagen, Denmark. Introduced 1958. Parentage: Masquerade × (Poulsen's Bedder × Floradora).

SANDER'S WHITE RAMBLER White 10ft climber

Very vigorous; climber, with very pendulous shoots, easy to train; very healthy; foliage very abundant, tiny leaves set close, very glossy, bright deep green; flowers white with yellow stamens; semi-double, opening to 1½ins diameter, with 20 petals in rosette type, loose-centred flower; very profuse summer flower, not much thereafter; flowers in large clusters, average 12 to 20 per stem, on side shoots growing from wood made in former years; weather resistance fair; sweet scent.
Raised by Sander & Son, St Albans, Hertfordshire. Introduced 1912. Parentage: Unknown.

SCABROSA Rosy magenta 4ft shrub

Very vigorous; shrub, branching out to form a dense bush wider than high, many bristly thorns; very healthy; foliage very abundant, glossy, bright green, handsome, starts appearing early in year; flowers bright rose magenta, showing superb yellow stamens while young, succeeded by large tomato-red heps; single, large, opening to 5ins diameter, with 5 petals, occasionally 7; profuse summer bloom, with very good continuity of incidental flower to autumn; flowers in clusters of several heads, opening in succession; weather resistance fairly good; rich and sweet scent.
Origin unknown; it appears likely that it is an improved form of *R. rugosa rubra* discovered by R. Harkness & Co. Ltd, Hitchin, Hertfordshire. Introduced 1950.

SCARLET QUEEN ELIZABETH Scarlet 4ft bush

Very vigorous; bush, upright and branching out freely; healthy; foliage abundant, fairly glossy, darkish green; flowers bright scarlet, fading to pinkish scarlet; double, opening to 3½ins diameter, tending to be round at centre, with 30 petals; very abundant bloom summer to autumn, with good few between flushes; flowers usually 3 to 7 per stem, sometimes in larger heads; weather resistance good; scent faint but sweet.

Raised by Patrick Dickson, Newtownards, Northern Ireland. Introduced 1963. Parentage: (Korona × seedling) × Queen Elizabeth.

SCHARLACHGLUT   Scarlet 7ft shrub

Very vigorous; shrub, with long shoots arching over, making a plant of open formation, spreading wider than high, could be trained as climber; very healthy; foliage ample, semi-glossy, deep green; flowers bright scarlet, showing yellow stamens, and succeeded by large red heps; single, opening to 3½ins diameter, with 5 petals; profuse summer flower, hardly any thereafter; flowers in clusters on side shoots arising from old wood; a number of these borne along the arching branches can be quite spectacular; weather resistance good; faint scent.
Raised by Wilhelm Kordes, Sparrieshoop, Germany. Introduced 1952. Parentage: Poinsettia × Alika. Sometimes listed as Scarlet Fire.

SCHNEEZWERG   White 5ft shrub

Very vigorous; shrub, upright, spreading into a good, broad plant; very healthy; foliage small, very abundant, fairly glossy, light to middle green; flowers white, showing yellow stamens; semi-double, opening flat to about 2½ins diameter, with about 16 petals; profuse summer bloom, followed by more scattered flowers into autumn; flowers in clusters of 3 to 12 per stem; weather resistance fair; sweet scent.
Raised by Peter Lambert, Trier, Germany. Introduced 1912. Parentage: Unknown. Also known as Snow Dwarf.

SEA PEARL   Peach pink/yellow 4ft bush

Very vigorous; bush, decidedly upright, with sufficient shoots to make a substantial plant; some rust; foliage abundant, glossy, coppery dark green; flowers are variable in colour, sometimes orange carmine fading salmon pink with pearly cream base; or at other times much softer pink, with peach pink reverse, and cream yellow base; the old flowers become pale, with red flecks; double, opening to 4ins diameter, with 22 large petals forming an elegant long flower, with attractive pointed centre; abundant bloom summer and autumn, with good supply between flushes; flowers in large heads on the stronger shoots,

and singly or in small groups on the side shoots; weather
resistance good; faint sweet scent.
Raised by Patrick Dickson, Newtownards, Northern Ireland.
Introduced 1964. Parentage: Perfecta × Montezuma.

SHEPHERD'S DELIGHT   Orange red 3ft bush

Very vigorous; bush, spreading well, basically upright; healthy;
foliage very abundant, glossy, dark green, handsome; flowers
open very bright rich deep orange, with some carmine coming
in as the flowers age; semi-double, opening to 2ins diameter,
with 15 petals, rather untidy form, open centre; very abundant
flower summer and autumn, with some between flushes;
flowers in large heads, occasionally in small clusters; weather
resistance fair; faint scent.
Raised by Alex. Dickson & Sons Ltd, Newtownards, Northern
Ireland. Introduced 1956. Parentage: Masquerade seedling ×
Joanna Hill.

SHOT SILK   Salmon/yellow 2ft bush

Vigorous; bush, upright, of low compact habit; healthy; foliage
abundant, glossy, middle green, very fresh and attractive;
flowers salmon pink, shaded yellow, quite sparkling, not fading
much; double, opening to 4½ins diameter, with 26 petals, very
attractive centre, soon opening; profuse flower summer and
autumn, repeating well between flushes; flowers produced
singly, or 3 to 5 per stem, rarely in large heads; weather
resistance excellent; rich lemon scent.
Raised by Alex. Dickson & Sons Ltd, Newtownards, Northern
Ireland. Introduced 1924. Parentage: Hugh Dickson seedling
× Sunstar.

SIR GALAHAD   Red 2ft bush

Vigorous; bush, spreading readily to form a neat, well-balanced
plant; healthy; foliage abundant, semi-glossy, medium green;
flowers open red, the centre lighter red, do not fade much;
semi-double, opening to 2½ins diameter, very neatly formed
with attractive straight centre, clean and pleasant outline to
petals of which there are 23; very abundant flowers summer to
autumn, giving 3 flushes, with some flowers between; flowers
in well-spaced clusters of 5 to 7, sometimes forms large heads,

more rarely less than 5 to a stem; weather resistance excellent; slight scent.
Raised by R. Harkness & Co. Ltd, Hitchin, Hertfordshire. Introduced 1967. Parentage: Pink Parfait × Highlight.

SIR LANCELOT   Apricot yellow 2½ft bush

Vigorous; bush, upright, quite willing to spread outwards, not always compactly; some mildew and blackspot; foliage ample, glossy, light to middle green; flowers open apricot, or more apricot yellow in hot weather, quite a unique colour, very pure; old flowers fade pale with red flecks; semi-double, very pretty bud form, opening to 3½ins diameter, and showing stamens; 18 petals; profuse flower summer and autumn, some between flushes; flowers in clusters of 3 to 12, close together, or in large heads on main shoots; weather resistance good; slight scent.
Raised by R. Harkness & Co. Ltd, Hitchin, Hertfordshire. Introduced 1967. Parentage: Vera Dalton × Woburn Abbey.

STANWELL PERPETUAL   Blush 3ft bush

Vigorous; bush, very thorny, grows compact, dense and upright, but the stems are not stiff, and arch out when weighted with flower; healthy; foliage small, abundant, matt, grey green, giving plant airy appearance in spite of the density of stems; flowers blush, fading white; double, opening to 2½ins diameter, with many small petals, folded and lying flat round the centre; profuse in summer then has a succession of a few flowers at a time to the autumn; flowers in small clusters; weather resistance moderate; sweet scent.
Raised by J. Lee, Hammersmith, Middlesex. Introduced 1838. Parentage: *R. damascena semperflorens* × *R. spinosissima.*

STELLA   Pink 3ft bush

Vigorous; bush, upright, spreading out easily; healthy; foliage abundant, glossy, light to middle green; flowers open with light pink centre, the outer petals deeper pink, fading paler when old; double, opening to 5ins diameter, with 40 petals forming a large flower, the centre regular, straight, stately, holding closed to a late stage; abundant flower summer and autumn, some between flushes; flowers borne 3 to 7 per shoot,

rarely singly, quite frequently in large heads; weather resistance excellent; slight, sweet scent.
Raised by Mathias Tantau, Uetersen, Germany. Introduced 1958. Parentage: Horstmann's Jubilaumsrose × Peace.

STERLING SILVER   Lilac pink 2ft bush

Weak; bush, with upright growth, not many shoots; healthy; foliage sparse, medium green, leaves rather rounded, semi-glossy; flowers light lilac with pink underlying the colour, fades paler with age; interesting as a step towards a blue rose, not particularly attractive in the garden, but can be very fine grown under glass; double, opening to 4ins diameter (or smaller when flowering in trusses), with 30 petals, excellent symmetric heart to the flower; flowers summer and autumn, freely in proportion to the vigour; often flowers in heads of many flowers, but is more attractive flowering one per stem, and therefore worth disbudding; weather resistance poor; scent very sweet and pleasant.
Raised by Mrs Gladys Fisher, Woburn, Massachusetts, USA. Introduced 1957. Parentage: Seedling × Peace.

SUMMER SUNSHINE   Yellow 3ft bush

Vigorous; bush, rather open in habit, upright and spreading out with long side shoots; some blackspot; foliage moderately abundant, semi-glossy, middle green; flowers strong brilliant yellow, not fading much; double, opening to 4½ins diameter, well formed cone at centre, opening rather quickly, 26 petals; very profuse in flower summer and autumn, some between flushes; produces flowers one to a stem, or 3 to 5, sometimes in large heads; weather resistance good; sweet scent.
Raised by H. C. Swim for Armstrong Nurseries, Ontario, California, USA. Introduced 1962. Parentage: Buccaneer × Lemon Chiffon. Known in France as Soleil d'Ete.

SUPER STAR   Light scarlet 3ft bush

Very vigorous; bush, upright and spreading out into a fine large plant; some mildew; foliage moderately abundant, glossy, darkish green; flowers clear pale scarlet, particularly luminous, fading with mauve edges when old; double, opening to 4ins diameter, extremely well formed and regular flower, straight, handsome centre, 36 petals; very prolific summer and autumn flower, many between flushes; flowers usually start with a single terminal bloom per stem, then many in the side shoots, generally 3 to 5 per stem, occasionally in a large head; weather resistance good; sweet if light scent.

Raised by Mathias Tantau, Uetersen, Germany. Introduced 1960. Parentage: (seedling × Peace) × (seedling × Alpine Glow). Also known as Tropicana.

SUTTER'S GOLD   Yellow/pink 3ft bush

Vigorous; bush, upright, with a decided lateral spread by the side shoots; healthy; foliage rather sparse, glossy, dark green; flowers from orange buds, opening light yellow with pink tinges, a little paler when old; double, opening to $4\frac{1}{2}$ins diameter, with 22 petals, most attractive form when opening and while centre holds closed; very profuse summer and autumn flower, some between flushes; weather resistance fairly good; flowers borne 1 to 5 per stem, occasionally more; strong lemon scent.

Raised by H. C. Swim for Armstrong Nurseries, Ontario, California, USA. Introduced 1950. Parentage: Charlotte Armstrong × Signora.

SUZON LOTTHÉ   Pale pink 3ft bush

Vigorous; bush, decidedly upright, spreading moderately, smooth stems; healthy; foliage abundant, semi-glossy, dark green; flowers very pale pink, with deeper colour at petal edges, does not fade much; double, opening to 5ins diameter, with 35 petals, very well formed flower with long lasting cone at centre; fairly profuse summer and autumn flower, some between flushes; weather resistance fair; rich sweet scent.

Raised by Francis Meilland, Cap d'Antibes, France. Introduced 1951. Parentage: Peace × (Signora × Mrs John Laing).

THE FAIRY   Pink 3ft shrub

Vigorous; shrub, spreading wide as the growth is rather lax, likely to be slow reaching full height, but flowering well while small; very healthy; foliage very abundant, close set, small, very glossy, deep green; flowers soft fresh pink, fading paler;

double, opening about 1½ins diameter, with many small petals in pretty rosette shape; very abundant flower in summer and autumn with generous amount between flushes; flowers in large heads; weather resistance good; light scent.
Discovered by J. A. Bentall, Havering-atte-Bower, Essex. Introduced 1932. Parentage: Sport of Lady Godiva.

TRAUMLAND   Pink 1½ft bush

Vigorous; bush, neat and spreading low growth; healthy; foliage abundant, glossy, dark green; flowers light rose pink, a little paler with age; semi-double, with open centre, 3ins diameter, flat flower of 16 petals neatly arrayed; very profuse summer and autumn flower, some between flushes; flowers in heads of 5 to 12 normally; weather resistance good; sweet scent.
Raised by Mathias Tantau, Uetersen, Germany. Introduced 1959. Parentage: Tantau's Surprise × Fashion. Also known as Dreamland.

VERA DALTON   Pink 2½ft bush

Vigorous; bush, upright but spreading outwards with rather open habit; slight mildew; foliage fairly abundant, shiny, dark green; flowers rose pink, a little paler with age; semi-double, opening to 3½ins diameter, with 30 petals, very attractive both when young with closed, symmetric centre, and when wide as a beautiful open blossom; very free bloom summer and autumn with some between; flowers in large heads, blooms held well apart, sometimes 3 to 9 to a stem; weather resistance good; pleasant scent.
Raised by Albert Norman, Normandy, Surrey. Introduced 1961. Parentage: Paul's Scarlet Climber self-set seedling × (Mary × Queen Elizabeth).

VIOLET CARSON   Pink 2½ft bush

Vigorous; bush, upright and spreading to make a wide, handsome plant; slight mildew; foliage fairly abundant, semi-glossy, dark green with coppery tinge; flowers light pink, with salmon flush, rather variable, paler when old; double, opening to 3½ins diameter; 40 petals in tight formation, good, straight centre; abundant flower summer and autumn, good few between flushes; flowers in very large heads on the main shoots, 3 to 7 on side shoots; weather resistance fair; light sweet, scent. Raised by Sam McGredy, Portadown, Northern Ireland. Introduced 1964. Parentage: Mme Leon Cuny × Spartan.

VIOLINISTA COSTA   Pink 2ft bush

Vigorous; bush, with determined outward spread; mildew likely; foliage abundant, very glossy, dark green; flowers deep pink, with reddish salmon shading, yellow deep in centre, a little lighter when old; double, with well formed flowers, soon opening wide, to 4½ins diameter, 36 petals; flowers very freely summer to autumn, some between flushes; bears its blooms usually 3 to a stem, and spaces them very well over the bush; weather resistance good; sweet scent.
Raised by Rosas Camprubi, Barcelona, Spain. Introduced 1936. Parentage: Sensation × Shot Silk.

WENDY CUSSONS   Rose red 3ft bush

Very vigorous; bush, upright, spreading out robustly; healthy; foliage abundant, middle to deep green, fairly glossy; flowers when young rose red, opening to what most people would call deep pink; double, opening to 5ins diameter, with 35 petals, well formed cone at centre; very profuse summer and autumn bloom, good number between flushes; flowers 1 to 3 per stem, sometimes more; weather resistance fairly good; strong lemon scent.
Raised by C. Gregory & Son Ltd, Chilwell, Nottingham. Introduced 1959. Parentage: Thought to be Independence × Eden Rose.

WOBURN ABBEY   Orange 3ft bush

Vigorous; bush, strong upright shoots, spreading out moderately; liable to get mildew and rust; foliage abundant, close set, glossy, light green; flowers tangerine, showy, turning to orange pink, fading; double, opening to 2½ins diameter, with 30 petals forming tight straight centre while young (centre sometimes split), showing stamens later; very abundant in bloom summer and autumn, some between flushes; flowers in large heads on main shoots, 3 to 9 on side shoots; weather resistance fair; light, sweet scent.

Raised by G. Sidey, Earl Shilton, Leicestershire. Introduced 1962. Parentage: Masquerade × Fashion.

ZÉPHIRINE DROUHIN   Pink 10ft climber

Vigorous; climber, with almost thornless branches, easy to train; some mildew; foliage abundant, matt, coppery light green; flowers deep rose pink, a little lighter with age; semi-double, opening to 3ins diameter, with 20 petals, the centre often quartered in an attractive way; very free flowering in summer, almost a constant succession of flowers somewhere on the plant to autumn; flowers usually 3 to 12 on side shoots from wood of former years, also on new growths; weather resistance fairly good; rich lemon scent.

Raised by Bizot, France. Introduced 1868. Parentage: Not known.

13 On enjoyment

At the start of this book, I placed the reader in a deck chair, but he was not there very long. No, I soon had him out of it, digging and planting and pruning. Those things are done now, and it is time to relax again, to take stock of what we have admitted into our lives by interesting ourselves in roses, and to consider the prospects ahead.

It might well be emphasized again that this book aims to set forth essential principles, and to explain the reasons for them. By no means does it explore the many interesting studies and more painstaking skills which lie hidden behind the beguiling blossoms of the rose.

For beguiling they are; in planting roses, you have laid yourself open to the anxieties of all who grow plants; but also to the joys of producing by yourself the most lovely thing that any man can see: when roses bloom, they speak to you in the accents of perfection. You will remember individual flowers as long as your life continues. You will find pleasure even in the thorns. You will want to know more about your roses.

In that event, the first sensible step is to join the Royal National Rose Society. The Society lives in a converted country house at Bone Hill, Chiswell Green Lane, St Albans. It started in 1876, due to the energies of Dean Hole, a distinguished Victorian clergyman; and it is now a body of over one hundred thousand members. All members receive publications which contain sensible guidance, namely, *Hints on Cultivation*, a *Select List of Roses* thought to be the best, and a *Rose Annual*. The first two are supplied to members on enrolment, and subsequently as revised from time to time. But the *Annual* arrives every March, and anyone with a collection of *Annuals* has a wealth of information to hand. They give the latest news on new roses, as well as interesting articles on all aspects of the rose. Not the least valuable feature is the Rose Analysis, in which the votes of a number of members are canvassed, in order to discover which varieties they find best for various purposes. These are tabulated, so that the *Annual* is able to publish tables, like the football league tables in the newspapers, delivering a consensus of opinion in concise form.

The Society runs a Summer and Autumn Rose Show in London, and a Provincial Show in conjunction with a Society elsewhere in the country; for the past few years in Leeds. To any lover of roses, the Rose Society's shows ought to be a magnet.

At St Albans, on the Society's own land, is a Trial Ground, where new varieties from all over the world are tested. Awards are made to those proving most worthy, under an exacting and careful system of judging.

For these services, and others I have not mentioned, the Society charges a modest subscription of one guinea.

You may become an exhibitor at shows, if your fancy lies that way; and if so, you will soon find your list of friends will grow. Or you may become interested in some special types of roses. Perhaps you will master the art of propagation, or even that of breeding new roses. If your bent is research, the history and development of roses may attract you. If you are practical, you will be studying methods of feeding, results from your pruning, and from every operation that is done to roses. You can even make rose-petal wine; 'Peace' makes a delicious white wine, 'Fragrant Cloud' is rose, and 'Ena Harkness' red. I am anxious to persuade my wife to experiment with more varieties, but she has become keen on taking photographs of roses just at the moment. She wants to build up a collection of them, and as we have over one thousand varieties, it is going to cost me an awful lot to keep her in film.

Do you see how many fascinating branch lines are extending into the future? I am afraid that you are in great danger of being led along one or more of them. But this book is not made to accompany you. This books deals with the beginning only. Its scope is over, its purpose, I hope, to some degree accomplished, except for one last plea: please enjoy your roses. Get some fun out of them. Don't go all serious and solemn over them. They are tough plants, needing firmness, common sense, a little under-standing. The pests and diseases that attack them are not as a general rule liable to kill them, for they have a vested interest in keeping the rose alive. Nature, being impartial, wants both mildew and rose to flourish. All we have discussed in this book is designed to make the roses strong and fit to stand their troubles more easily.

Relax now in your deck chair. Let us spend these last few pages in one of the great pleasures of a rose grower's life—memories of happy incidents.

I remember taking Robert to his first Autumn Show. Robert is my elder son. He was, I believe, nine years of age, and a veteran with three years' experience on the nursery, when I took him to the Autumn Show. He fetched and carried, filled tubes with water, until the work was nearly done; and then it was very late, about 3 am. He slept a while on a Lilo in the exhibition hall, and woke fresh as a daisy about an hour later. In the early daylight, as Robert and I were inspecting other people's exhibits, we met Mr Harry Wheatcroft, who is to the rose trade what P. T. Barnum was to the circus trade. 'And who is this?' asked Harry, seeing the boy. Proudly, as any parent with a fine son, I replied, 'This is Robert Harkness.' Harry, a memorable figure, tall, powerful, with flowing hair, bushy whiskers and clothes you could pick out in a crowd on a foggy day, bent down to the boy and shook hands with him in the nicest avuncular way imaginable. He said, 'Robert Harkness, I am happy to meet you. Do you know, you have the *second* best name in rose growing.'

I remember the girls in our office trying to read customers' signatures. It is a strange thing that customers cannot sign their names clearly. They write PEACE and ENA HARKNESS in bold capitals, lest we should make a mistake. If they scrawled Pce and EH we should know what they meant. But we have no such insight into the squiggle that usually follows 'Yours faithfully'. Girls are human, apt to misconstrue when they are working fast. An unfortunate misconstruction answered a letter, beautifully typed, from an eminent naval officer. 'Yours faithfully,' it ended, 'squiggle, Vice Admiral.' The reply went to V. Admiral Esq. Yes, girls are only human, praise be.

I remember our fertilizer trial. We decided to satisfy our curiosity as to the efficiency of various recommended fertilizers. So we purchased them, and applied them to every fourth row of roses in the nursery. We put a small label against each row so treated. As the summer wore on, we thought it well to continue the trials. Therefore on some of the treated rows we put another application of fertilizer, sometimes the same as it had before, sometimes different. We wrote on the labels what we had done. In the autumn, as we looked over the field, to evaluate this permutation of fertilizer trials, we could not see a bit of difference anywhere, whether treated or not. But we had an order from a lady who had obviously seen the labels. She asked for 6 Ena Harkness and 6 Blood and Fish.

I remember so many incidents, so many grand people in roses, so many varieties, flowers, individual plants. I remember days in the rose field, when if the back ached, the heart still burst with thanks; I remember a very distinguished Siamese visitor.

When he came, it happened that a friend from Singapore was staying with me. We showed the Siamese gentleman round the nursery, and I listened, quite delighted, to the following conversation:

Siam: What do you do in Singapore, with those unpleasant insects who come out at night, and walk up your rose stems biting off every leaf they see, so that in the morning you come out into the garden and see nothing but leafless stalks?

Singapore: Oh, that is easy. All you need is a box of dung. You put it in the bed one evening. These creatures have depraved tastes. They will all go into the box of dung instead of attacking your roses.

Siam: Splendid! You have caught them! All you need do is put the box of dung on the fire next day and destroy them utterly!

Singapore: No, no, no, no! You give the box of dung to the gardener and tell him to pick the insects out and destroy them. Then you can use the same box of dung the next evening.

I remember a gentleman from the government who came to the nursery to fill in a form. When he got to the line saying 'Date', he was at a loss for a moment. He said, 'I say, what is the date to-day?' '29 October,' he was told. With that he put down his pen, and disappeared into the office lavatory. The witty member of the firm looked at the closed door: 'Must be an annual affair,' he remarked.

I remember so many pleasant things that I had better exercise some self-discipline and stop recounting them. Yet I feel it would be a pity to end this chapter without mentioning Barney Brannigan.

It was Gordon Forsyth who acted as midwife. Gordon is editor of *Popular Gardening*, and gardening correspondent to the *Daily Telegraph*. He asked me to write on roses for *Popular Gardening*. I thought this over for some time, and I came to the conclusion that it would be more fun to convey the dry stuff of instruction by lightening the scene with some fictitious characters. Of these, Barney Brannigan is the chief; he is an Irishman with a proper native disregard for established rules. This was a departure for a serious gardening paper, especially in the hands of an amateur writer, but Gordon Forsyth had faith in Barney and his creator, and so the series ran along quite happily.

I have often been asked where I met Barney. The answer is that I lived in Ireland for a while, and when I was there I heard a story, which I elaborated a little, and wrote. I put Barney Brannigan into it, little supposing that he should turn up in *Popular Gardening* in the future. And as the story was of a previous generation, it is obvious that it must apply to one of the present Barney's forebears, quite naturally of the same name.

So I end this book with the memory of Barney, for I have a horror of the modern monomania, the idea that one becomes absorbed in one thing for its own sake. However absorbing, any one interest is a part of life, not the whole of it; an addition to life, not a substitute for it. Roses, like all good things in this world, are fit company for laughter, and good fellowship; enrichers of a full life, multipliers of the happiness of the human race; a golden part of life, but not life's whole.

Index

Index

YOUR ADDITIONS TO THE ROSE LIST

VARIETY	DESCRIPTION

YOUR ADDITIONS TO THE ROSE LIST

VARIETY	DESCRIPTION

YOUR ADDITIONS TO THE ROSE LIST

VARIETY	DESCRIPTION

YOUR ADDITIONS TO THE ROSE LIST

VARIETY	DESCRIPTION

YOUR ADDITIONS TO THE ROSE LIST

VARIETY	DESCRIPTION

YOUR ADDITIONS TO THE ROSE LIST

VARIETY	DESCRIPTION

YOUR ADDITIONS TO THE ROSE LIST

VARIETY	DESCRIPTION

YOUR ADDITIONS TO THE ROSE LIST

VARIETY	DESCRIPTION